Emotional Leadership

*****

Helpful Lessons Will Teach You How To Becoming an Efficient Leader. How To Influence People. Emotional Intelligence For Leadership. An Executive Leader Is Also A Decision Maker

By: DR. Felicity Gray

Contents

Introduction

Leadership is a popular topic today. People are simply fascinated by who leaders are and what they do. They want to be aware of what really accounts for exceptional leadership and how to become one in the process. However, in spite of this strong attention in leadership, there are books that describe the right means of practicing leadership. In addition, this book about Emotional Leadership will help fill that void.

Each chapter describes an essential leadership principle and how each one relates in practice to become an efficient leader.

Everyone, in one way or another, is asked to lead, whether in the classroom, in a soccer team, in a glee club, in work, or even in fundraising events. There are many situations in life where leadership is required. A leader can be both high profile just like an elected public official, or low profile or those you see in the workplace, at school, and in the community who take the initiative for change. However, take note that there will be situations in life where leadership is demanded on someone who takes the role of a leader.

Being a leader is both challenging and rewarding. It goes with it loads of responsibilities. Leadership is believed to be both an ability and a trait. It is a trait because it puts emphasis on a leader's special gifts. If you are aware of the old dictum "Leaders are born, not made" then you will understand what this said gift is. While some would disagree with this because it implies that only those given special talents have the right to lead,   there is still some truth to this argument.

Leadership is also said to be an ability. While this term refers to a natural capacity, this can also be acquired. Take, for instance, there are people who are born good at speaking in public, but there are also those who only become comfortable and good when they begin to study and practice speaking in public.

This book will help you learn more about what leadership is all about. Remember, the way you perceive leadership will have a great impact on how you practice it.

Chapter 1 – Leadership

Leadership Definition

The words "leader" and "leadership" can bring about a variety of images to one's mind. Leadership could mean a company executive who is busy developing his company to beat competitors; it could also mean a political leader who is chasing after his political dreams; or an explorer who tries to lead a small group of people to different kinds of adventures.

Leaders help others do the right thing. They are the ones who set the path, lead the way, build a vision, and set goals. When you're a leader, you are the one responsible for mapping out the direction of your team. But as you set the directions of your whole team's sail, it is also important that you make use of management skills to show your followers to the right destination in the most efficient and smoothest way possible.

In this chapter, we'll focus on what leadership is all about, how it works, and an in depth understanding of what it really is.

There are many definitions of leadership, but they can be sufficed through the following words:

- Leadership encourages and inspires members to do their own share in solving a particular problem.
- Leadership is adaptive. This means that a leader makes the necessary adjustments. Without said changes, followers may lose their way.
- Leadership is a skill. While talent is said to be an innate ability, skill on the other hand, can be gained through consistent training. You are also able to hone it through experience. Finally, persistence, makes for a great and able leader.
- Leadership empowers. This means that leaders are able to stimulate confidence and encourage self-assurance. There are different ways in which you inspire others. For one, you inspire by example, by bold or soft talk.
- Leadership performs on a setting. What this means is that a leader changes the state of the people and their surroundings. A leader cautiously watches those situations and conditions, and identifies the consequences contemplating on how to get a feel of the setting most effectively.
- Leadership loves progress. There is nothing more demotivating for a leader than the prospect of being stuck in a kind of environment where progress is not possible. Remember, if you can't move things forward, that's a sign that it is time to move on.

If you want progress to take place, there must be change. If an organization is expecting progress, change must happen. In due time, it must change into something different. It must become more relevant, better, and more strategic. Leaders are expected to test the process because most businesses and organizations will automatically conspire to maintain status quo, and as much as possible, avoid change. As a leader, you are expected to inspire progress and change among your members.

- Leadership is proactive. This means that as a leader, you have the ability to solve problems, look ahead, and not be content with what things are at the present moment. The moment you have designed your visions, you must make them convincing so that people can understand, see, and embrace said visions.

- Leadership requires courage. A leader must be the first person to step out in a new path or direction. And being the first to step outside of the zone requires courage. In this light, courage creates leadership.

This principle has been at work ever since we were children. Remember standing around with your friends, daring each other to do something out of the ordinary? Then suddenly, you saw somebody doing it first and then everybody followed suit? That person who went first is generally deemed as a leader. And given that leader's initiative made others around him have the courage to follow as well.

There are many definitions of leadership, and the more you know about it, the faster you grow to become a leader yourself. Learning from different experiences in life, whether it be small or big, enable you to become an effective one in whatever field you are in.

If you want to become an effective leader, you should follow these five concepts:

1. *First, there should be competence.* Leaders must have the capacity to channel their positive energies toward areas of leadership where they have the tendency to excel and progress more.

2. *Second, a leader must be courageous.* A leader doesn't necessarily have to be the smartest nor the most creative. A leader is one who possesses courage to initiate in order to see things in action and move ahead. A leader is someone who has the ability to put his feet forward even if the road seems uncertain. He shows bravery and determination.

3. *Third, there must be clarity.* Uncertainties often necessitate clear directives from those who lead. A leader

must learn how to clear instructions even if he is not certain about it.

4. *Fourth, leadership accepts mentorship.* You may be good, but without a mentor, you will never be as good and as effective as you can be.

5. *Finally, to become a good leader means to have the ability to see and own what you are really doing, thinking, and feeling.* This helps you expand your repertoire of strategies to cope and function in your chosen field.

Top 5 Characteristics of a Leader

Many studies have already been conducted in order to identify the traits of effective leaders. The results have produced quite a long list of leadership traits with each trait contributes to the leadership process. However, these findings raise a vital question: given that there are a good number of important leadership traits, which ones should a person who aims to become an effective leader embody? While the answer to this question is not clear, the following are five traits that can help you:

1. Confidence

Confident leaders are assured that what they are doing are all for the benefit of those whom they lead. This is a kind of trait that has something to do with your will to succeed and feel good about yourself. Your confidence should come from knowing what is expected and required of you. For example, when first learning to drive a car, a student's confidence is low because he does not know what to do or how to make the car run. If an instructor explains the driving process and demonstrates how to drive, the student can gain confidence because he now has an understanding of how to drive a car.

Understanding and awareness of oneself create a major confidence-booster. If you know yourself well, it is easier to display confidence. Apart from this, it is also important to have a good role model that you can look up to. This is why it is important to have a mentor who will guide you and provide constructive criticisms. This mentor may be an experienced coworker, a boss, or a friend from outside the organization. Mentors play the part of being good role models and provide essential help to learn the dynamics of leadership.

Confidence also comes from experience and continuous practice. Consider the best athletes in the world like Roger Federer, Serena Williams, and Tiger Woods among others. They all spend enormous hours practicing. Their confidence and excellent game are a result of not just their gifts and talents, but consistent practice as well.

In leadership, confidence is effectively built. Taking on leadership roles, even minor ones on committees or through volunteer activities, provide practice for being a leader. Building one leadership activity on another can increase confidence for more demanding leadership roles. Those who take on chances to practice their leadership will gain more knowledge and confidence in bettering their ability to lead.

2. Determination

Determination is another characteristic of an effective leader. Determined leaders are attentive to tasks and are focused. Determination is the decision to get the job done that includes characteristics such as persistence, initiative, and drive. Being determined means showing dominance at times, especially in situations where others need guidance.

We all have heard of determined people who were able to accomplish marvelous things – the single mom who was able to send her seven children to college, the blind woman who was able to conquer her disability and live just how a normal person would, a cancer patient who managed to climb the highest mountain like a pro. We have all encountered a person who is determined, and this is considered one of the most salient characteristics a leader should possess.

3. Integrity

Integrity describes leaders who are trustworthy and honest. When we are children, we were told not to tell a lie. For leaders, the lesson is the same: "Always be honest."

Dishonesty creates mistrust, and leaders who are not honest are deemed unreliable. Honesty helps people to have trust and faith in what leaders have to say and what they stand for. Honesty enhances a leader's ability to influence others because they have confidence and belief in their leader.

Truthfulness stresses the point of being open with others and embodying reality as completely as possible. However, this is not an easy task: there are instances when being honest and bold about something could be counterproductive, or in other cases, damaging. The real challenge is that a leader must know how to balance between being honest about it and observe what is suitable to reveal given a specific situation. While it is important for leaders to be genuine and trustworthy, it is also essential for them to have integrity in their relationships with others.

Integrity undergirds all aspects of leadership. It is at the core of being a leader. A leader's capacity to influence is often centered to how his integrity is presented to many people. If you fail to get the trust of your subordinates, your influence won't be considered effective.

4. Intelligence

Intelligence is another important characteristic of a leader. It includes perceptual skills, reasoning ability, and good language skills – all these make for better leaders.

There are many ways to improve one's intelligence even if it is difficult to alter one's IQ. Intelligent leaders are well informed. They are aware of what is going on around them and understand the job that needs to be done. It is a vital part in leadership to get hold of information as to what leadership role is required and to learn about their work environment. This information will help leaders be more knowledgeable and insightful.

While majority of people have average intelligence, becoming more knowledgeable about leadership gives us the information we need to become better leaders.

5. Charisma

This gets the most attention among all the important characteristics of leadership. It is referred to as special appeal and charm that can be a great contribution to how a person leads. Charisma is an extraordinary characteristic that gives a leader the power to do extraordinary things. Succinct to say, it gives a leader extraordinary influence.

Charisma is not a common personality trait, so it's a bit challenging to possess this. There are a few select people who are very charismatic, and then there's the rest who are not. Since not everyone possesses charisma, it often leads to the question, what do leaders have to do if they are not charismatic.

There are some behaviors that describe charismatic leadership:

- First, charismatic leaders show competence in every aspect of leadership. Therefore, many people rely to them to do most of the decision-making.
- Second, charismatic leaders act as exceptional role models for the kind of principles and beliefs that they want others to emulate. Think of a famous person who was able to influence and inspire others simply because of their charisma.
- Third, charismatic leaders communicate high expectations and show confidence to meet what is expected of them.
- Fourth, charismatic leaders articulate strong values and clear goals. It is by articulating one's dream that you are able to influence multitudes of people to follow peaceful practices.
- Finally, charismatic leaders are an inspiration to others. They motivate and inspire others to become truly engaged

in real change. They are salt to the earth, a good influence, and an exceptional role model.

Chapter 2 – Who is a Good Leader - Leadership Traits

What makes people leaders? Do leaders have certain qualities? These questions have been of interest for many. This chapter will address the traits that are important to leadership.

The list for effective leaders are aplenty. This includes, but are not limited to the following: dependability, diligence, meticulousness, self-assurance, trustworthiness, articulateness, sociability, open-mindedness, intelligence, and confidence. Because the list is so extensive, it is a bit challenging to find out exactly as to which traits are essential for leaders. When in fact, almost all these traits are connected to the qualities of a person who wish to lead.

When asked about leadership, what do you think are the most vital traits that a leader should possess? To answer this question, one must look into traits that appear to be strongly related to everyday life.

1. A good leader is sociable

Sociability is a leader's ability to create pleasant and amiable social relationships among people no matter their status in life. People want sociable leaders-leaders with whom they can get along with pretty easily. This should be leaders who show a friendly demeanor, is outgoing, tactful, and courteous. They are particularly understanding to people's needs, and display great concern for their well-being. Sociable leaders possess outstanding interpersonal skills that allow them to design a kind of workplace that is cooperative and friendly.

Being sociable comes easier for some than for others. For example, it is easy for extroverted leaders to talk to others and be outgoing, but it is harder for introverted leaders to do the same. Similarly, some individuals are naturally "people persons," while others prefer to be alone. Although people vary in the degree to which they are outgoing, it is possible to increase sociability. A sociable leader gets along with coworkers and other people in the work setting. Being friendly, kind, and thoughtful, as well as talking freely with others and giving them support, go a long way in order to establish a leader's sociability. Sociable leaders bring positive energy to a group and make the work environment a more enjoyable one.

2. A good leader knows his strengths

How are these strong points utilized in leadership? Even though practicing leadership does not have established theories, there are still a lot of useful applications that can be used in everyday leadership situations. There are several specific ways to incorporate strengths in your personal and work settings, and some are the following: developing your strengths, discovering your strengths, recognizing and engaging the strengths of others, and fostering a positive strength-based environment around you. Following these steps will not be a cure-all for becoming a perfect strength-based leader, but they will most certainly help you, as a leader, to maximize the use of your strengths.

Strengths can also emerge from your basic personality traits. We all have unique traits, and therefore we all have unique strengths. No one is without strengths. Extraordinary individuals are differentiated less by their remarkable 'raw power' rather than by their capacity to recognize their strengths ". The challenge we face is identifying these strengths and then employing them effectively.

Recognizing one's strengths is deemed as a distinctive challenge because most people often feel uncertain and even self-conscious about admitting their positive characteristics. This is because expressing one's strengths is often linked to being self-serving.

3. A good leader shows technical competence

This involves having specialized knowledge about the work you do or ask others to do. In the case of an organization, it includes understanding the intricacies of how an organization functions. A leader having specialized competency has administrative knowledge and understands the complex aspects of how the organization works.

For example, a school president should be well-versed when it comes to teaching, research, student recruitment, and student retention; a basketball coach should be knowledgeable about the basics of dribbling, passing, shooting, and rebounding; and a sales manager should have a thorough understanding of the product the salespeople are selling. Succinct to say, a leader is deemed more effective when one has technical competence about the activities all members are asked to perform.

Technical competence is sometimes referred to as "functional competence" because it means a person is competent in a particular function or area. No one is required to be competent in all avenues of life. However, you must keep in mind that you need not have technical competency every time. When you have technical skills, it means you are capable enough in a particular field specifically the one you are leading.

The importance of having technical competence can be well displayed in a business setting. A manager is the one who directs and supervises the business' dealings. In order to be more effective in this task, one must have the technical competence that pertains to business acumen, sales and marketing, and branding among others. Technical competence provides a manager the knowledge considered vital in administering members to perform together successfully.

4. A good leader should have interpersonal skills

Interpersonal skills are also known as people skills or a leader's ability to effectively work with subordinates, other superiors, and peers in order to achieve the objectives of the business or organization. While there are those who downplay the value of interpersonal skills or criticize them as inconsequential, leadership has constantly emphasized the importance of this skill to lead effectively.

To successfully lead an organization towards change, a leader needs to be sensitive to how his or her own ideas fit in with others' ideas. Social insightfulness is consists of having an understanding and awareness of how others are motivated, what is important to them, the challenges they face, and how they react to change. It includes a perception of the unique needs, goals, and demands of different organizational constituencies.

A leader given social insight has a good and precise idea of how his subordinates will act in response to any suggested modification in a company or organization. In essence, you can say that a socially perceptive leader can easily identify the pulse of employees on just about any issues.

Leadership is all about transformation, and those that are part of a group or organization often avoid change all because they have been more comfortable in the status quo. Novel ideas, different rules, or new ways of doing things are often seen as threatening because they do not fit in with how people are used to things being done. A socially perceptive leader has the power to establish change more efficiently if he is more familiar with how the planned and intended transformation may affect all the people concerned.

Another thing to consider is the emotional intelligence of a leader. Although EQ has materialized as an idea 20 years ago, it has already inspired interests among practitioners of leadership. Emotional intelligence is the ability of a person to comprehend his own emotions as well as other people, and then be able to apply said understanding to real life situations.

The fundamental basis of research on emotional intelligence is that those who are empathic of others' feelings and the impact their emotions have on others will be more effective leaders. Since showing emotional intelligence is positively related to effective leadership, what should a leader do to enhance his or her emotional skills?

Firstly, leaders must be sensitive of their own emotions, identify their feelings as they happen, and take their emotional pulse. Whether it is mad, glad, sad, or scared, a leader needs to assess constantly how he or she is feeling and what is causing those feelings.

Second, an effective leader must be taught to become sensitive of the emotions of others. A leader who knows how to read others' emotions is better equipped to respond appropriately to people's wants and needs. Stated another way, a leader needs to have empathy for others. He or she should understand the feelings of others as if those feelings were his or her own. This is why empathy is deemed as a crucial component of emotional intelligence.

Third, a leader must learn to control his emotions and makes sure that be able to apply them into good use. Whenever a leader makes an important decision, his emotions are involved. Therefore, emotions need to be embraced and managed for the good of the group or organization. When a leader is understanding of others' feelings, it increases the chances of having more effective and intelligent decisions among the group.

The key takeaway here is that people with emotional intelligence can easily recognize emotions and include this in what they do as leaders. To put simply, a leader that has high emotional intelligence always listens to his or her own feelings and that of others.

Conflict is inevitable. It creates the demand for change. In definition, conflict is a battle between people over alleged disagreements and disputes that concern issues such as following procedures, company rules, organizational regulations and the like.

When challenges arise, leaders and subordinates frequently feel unpleasant due to the stress, controversy, and strain that accompany it. Yes, this may be uncomfortable, but it doesn't necessarily mean that it is grave or serious. If oppositions and disagreements are properly resolved in effective and productive ways, the result is a reduction of stress, an increase in creative problem solving, and a strengthening of leader-follower and team-member relationships.

Addressing conflicts is never simple all because they are most certainly complicated. This is why it is important to provide a more thorough examination of the components of conflict and offer several practical communication approaches that a leader can take to constructively resolve differences.

Chapter 3 – Leadership and Followership

In a business or organization, there will always be people who do not identify themselves with the larger group, and this is considered to be one of the most difficult challenges facing a leader. When a leader fails to meet this challenge, these members feel devalued, and their unique contributions go unexpressed. Good leaders know the importance of listening to all members of a group, especially those who put themselves out of the circle.

Leadership and Followership entail that all group members, regardless if they are out-groups or not, should follow the one who leads them. It is common to find out-groups in any context where a group of individuals is trying to reach a goal. Out-groups are a natural occurrence in everyday life. They exist in all types of situations at the local, community, and national levels. In nearly all of these situations, when one or more individuals are not "on board" the performance of the group is adversely affected. Since out-group members are so common, it is important for anyone who aspires to be a leader to know how to work with them.

You will encounter almost all kinds of followers on a daily basis. At school, there are those kids who do not believe in joining a group or organization. They are either uncomfortable belonging to one or don't want to be ruled by someone their age. For instance, they may want to participate in sports, clubs, and so on, but for a host of reasons fail to do so.

At the workplace, you will encounter people who are always in disagreement with management's vision, or who are often left out from taking part in important decision-making roles.

In doing projects, there are those who refuse to make contributions and identify themselves as part of a group. On a broader level, in the United States, the Tea Party is an out-group that speaks for people who are disappointed with taxes and the government as a whole.

This chapter will examine why it is important for a leader to listen to this kind of group who refuses to belong, and how followership should always be part of leadership.

This discussion will emphasize on specific strategies that leaders can employ to build a sense of belongingness and community, and advance the goals of the larger group. There is a value implied in the direction taken, and that is that leaders have an obligation and a responsibility to listen to all members and be able to bring them into the circle should they feel outcast from the group.

Some will argue with this position, and others will say it is naive; but the unique inherent value of every single member of a group or an organization cannot go understated. Although there will be times when there are members who need to be abandoned because they are too extreme, it is inefficient to deal with them, or they just simply do not want to be included, leaders have a duty to listen and include them in the group no matter what.

Members who outcast themselves from the group can have many adverse effects on others. A number of disadvantages are comparatively irrelevant, such as bringing about slight incompetency and disorganizations in productivity. While there are those disadvantages that are rather significant, such as calling an industrial action or merely starting a conflict.

So why a leader should be concerned about the negative impact of this kind of members? First, they block what is supposed to be a harmonious work community. The essence of community is encouraging everyone to be on the same page and moving everyone in the same direction. Community brings people together and provides a place where they can express similar ideas, values, and opinions, and where they can be heard by members of their team. Community allows people to accomplish great things. It enables people to work hand in hand in pursuit of a shared vision that supports the common good. Through community, people can promote the greater good of everyone in the group.

However, by their very nature, out-group members are either in conflict with or avoiding community. Since they find the community they belong to be new and intimidating, there are those who opt to just get themselves out of the community. This action weakens the community, which is supposed to work hand in hand for a common goal.

A second reason that leadership should be concerned with out-groups is that they have a negative impact on teamwork and group collaboration. Group synergy is a kind of positive energy designed by group members who are working together for a common objective. It is an additive kind of energy that builds on itself. Group synergy is one of the most miraculous features of effective groups and of highly functioning teams. Groups with synergy accomplish far more than groups without it. Group synergy is not just the sum of each person's contribution; it is the sum of each person's contribution and then some. It is the "plus more" that allows high-functioning groups to achieve far beyond what would be expected.

Unfortunately, out-groups prevent groups from becoming synergistic and they remove group energy instead of providing more dynamism to the group. If out-group members are upset and demanding, they take even more energy from the group. This energy is not directed toward the goals of the group and so has a negative impact on productivity.

Rather than working together to accomplish a common goal, out-group members stand alone and seek to do their own thing. This is harmful for the group because the unique contributions of out-group members are not expressed, discussed, or utilized for the common good. Every person in a group brings singular talents and abilities that can benefit the group. When out-groups form, the individual contributions of some group members are not utilized, and group synergy is compromised.

A third reason why out-groups are a concern to the one who lead them is that they fail to obtain the respect they ought to have from other people. A central principle of leadership and followership is the duty to treat each member with respect. Remember, people need to be treated as autonomous individuals with their own goals, and not as the means to another person's goals. Being a leader means treating other people's decisions and values with respect: Failing to do so would signify that they are being treated as means to another's ends.

Leaders are still accountable to members who do not want to belong to a group. These people may have their own reason why they choose to not belong – either they feel unaccepted, aloof, alienated, or even discriminated. Whatever the reason is, a leader must still attend to them no matter what. Their voices still deserve to be heard.

In conclusion, the effect of these out group members is still considered significant. They may have a negative impact when it comes to group interaction, but a true leader must step up in such a way that will not separate out groups from the rest.

Executive leadership has an ethical aspect because leaders are the ones that influence the lives of his/her subordinates. Given this influential facet, leadership carries with it a huge responsibility. Hand in hand with the authority to make decisions is the obligation a leader has to use for the common good. Because the leader usually has more power and control over followers, they have to be particularly sensitive as to how their leadership affects the well-being of others.

Executive leadership is the ability to guide and influence employees. These leaders' typical day is done through constant overseeing of business processes as a means to fulfill organizational plans, goals, and overall decision making.

An executive leader moves his people to do the right thing, in the right way, and for the right reasons. Executive leadership is a kind of leadership where the good person rightfully influences others to achieve a common goal: to make the workplace more productive, better, and on the same boat.

An executive leader displays the kind of values and morals an individual or society finds desirable or appropriate. In leadership, it always has something to do with the leader's behavior, his very nature, and as well as his motives. This is because leaders every so often have great influence, power, and control over others, and the way they lead usually influences different organizations and individuals. Because of this, it is the leader's way of leading—

through his or her behavior, decisions, and interactions—that establish the atmosphere for a business or organization.

Executive leadership is also about the leader's actions. This refers to how a leader goes about achieving work goals. The way a leader goes about his or her work is a critical determinant of whether he or she is an effective executive leader. The actions a leader to achieve a goal need to be morally appropriate.

In everyday situations, a leader can act in many different ways to accomplish goals; each of these actions has ethical implications. For example, when a leader rewards some employees and not others, it raises questions of fairness. If a leader fails to take into consideration an employee's major health problems and instead demands that a job be completed on short notice, it raises questions about the leader's compassion for others. Even a simple task such as scheduling people's workload or continually giving more favorable assignments to one person over another reflects the ethics of the leader. In reality, almost everything a leader does has ethical overtones.

Given the importance of a leader's actions, what principles should guide how a leader acts toward others? Some of the principles for leaders have been described by many scholars. These writings highlight the importance of many standards.

In addition, there are three principles that have particular relevance to the actions of executive leaders. They are: respect, serve others, and show justice.

When you show respect, it means that you treat others' decisions and values with esteem. It also requires valuing others' ideas and affirming these individuals as unique human beings. When a leader shows respect to subordinates, subordinates become more confident and believe that their contributions have value.

Serving others is an example of altruism, an approach that suggests that actions are principled if their primary purpose is to promote the best interest of others. From this perspective, a leader may be called on to act in the interest of others, even when it may run contrary to his or her self-interests.

In the workplace, serving others can be observed in activities such as mentoring, empowering others, team building, and citizenship behaviors. To put this into practice, a leader must be eager to be follower-centered. That is, the leader tries to place others' interests foremost in his or her work, and act in ways that will benefit others.

Finally, justice. Executive leaders always make it a point that everyone is treated equally. There must be fairness with each and every decision done. Given this, no special treatment or any kind of consideration is given to a member. When each member of the group is treated in a different way, there must be some reasonable grounds for this, and it must be clear and based on sound values.

In addition, justice is concerned with the Golden Rule: Treat others as you would like to be treated. If you expect fair treatment from others, then you should treat others fairly. This particular issue has become problematic due to limited resources. As a result, there is often competition for scarce resources. Because of perceived scarcity, these disputes arise between people about reasonable methods of distribution. A leader must be able to clearly establish the rules for distributing rewards. This talks about the foundations of the leader and the business.

The Goals of the Leader

The goals that a leader sets up is based on how a rule influences members of an organization. Recognizing and practicing unbiased and valuable objectives are deemed as critical steps that an executive leader must embark on. In choosing goals, a leader must assess the relative value and worth of his or her goals. In the process, it is important for the leader to take into account the interests of others in the group or organization and, in some cases, the interests of the community and a larger culture in which he or she works. An executive leader attempts to create goals wherein all parties can agree mutually. A leader with the right goals will not impose his or her will on others.

The Executive Leader as Decision Maker

An executive leader is also a decision maker. Not only does he make decisions, rather he does armed with the right judgement. A leader has power because he or she has the ability to affect others' beliefs, attitudes, and courses of action. Religious leaders, managers, coaches, and teachers all have the potential to influence others. When they use their potentials, they are using their power as a resource to effect change in others.

Since power can be used in positive ways to benefit others or in destructive ways to hurt others, a leader needs to be aware and sensitive to how he or she uses power. Power is not fundamentally evil, however, most people use it in negative ways making it look bad. How an executive leader uses his power will have a great impact on how he makes decisions for the company or business.

In order to eliminate power abuse, it is important that everyone in a group or organization is aware and vigilant enough as to the kind of leadership the leader is showing. An ethical leader does not wield power or dominate, but instead takes into account the will of the subordinates, as well as the leader's own will. An ethical leader uses power to work with subordinates to accomplish mutual goals.

Another factor to consider to understanding executive leadership is values. These are beliefs, ideas, and manners of action that are meaningful and worthwhile. Some examples of values are peace. In leadership situations, both the leader and the follower have values, and these are seldom the same.

A leader brings his or her own unique values to leadership situations, and followers do the same. The challenge here is to be committed and reliable to one's leadership standards whilst being sensitive to your followers' own set of ethics and principles.

For example, a leader in an organization may value community and encourage his or her employees to work together and seek consensus in planning. However, the leader's subordinates may value self-expression and individuality. This creates a problem because these values are seemingly in conflict. In this situation, a leader needs to find a way to advance his or her own interests in creating community without destroying the subordinates' interests in individuality.

There is a tension between these different values; an executive leader needs to negotiate through these differences to find the best outcome for everyone involved. While the list of possible conflicts of values is infinite, finding common ground between a leader and followers is usually possible, and is essential to leadership and in decision making.

In the social services sector, where there are often too few resources and too many people in need, leaders constantly struggle with decisions that test their values. Because resources are limited, a leader has to decide where to allocate said resources. These decisions communicate a lot about the leader's values. For example, in mentoring programs. The list of children in need is often much longer than the list of available mentors. How do administrators decide which child is going to be assigned a mentor?

They decide based on their values and the values of the people with whom they work with. If they believe that children from households with only a single parent raising their family should have higher priority, then those children will be put at the top of the priority list. As this example illustrates, making decisions is challenging for a leader, especially in situations where resources are scarce.

An important factor when dealing with leadership and values is to understand ones own values and be able to integrate those values with others. This highlights the importance of a leader knowing his or her own values, having the courage to express them, and integrating these values into everyday decisions at work.

There is a strong demand for executive leaders with the right values today. Executive leadership is defined where a good leader acts in the right ways in order to achieve worthy goals.

There are six factors related this, some of them are the following:

1. First, character is fundamental to leadership. A leader's character refers to who he is as a person and his core values. A leader who is a decision maker should be trustworthy, responsible, fair, respectful, and caring.

2. Second, leadership is explained by the actions of the leader—the means a leader uses to accomplish goals. A leader engages in showing respect, serving others, and showing justice.

3. Third, leadership is about the goals of the leader. The goals a leader selects reflect his or her values. Selecting goals that are meaningful and worthwhile is one of the most important decisions a leader needs to make.

4. Fourth, leadership is concerned with the honesty of the leader. Without honesty, a leader cannot be a good leader and effective decision maker. In telling the truth, a leader needs to strike a balance between openness and sensitivity to others.

5. Fifth, power plays a role in leadership. A leader has an obligation to use power for the influence of the common good of others. The interests of subordinates need to be

taken into account, and the leader needs to work with subordinates to accomplish mutual ends.

6. Finally, leadership is concerned with the values of the leader. An ethical leader has strong morals and principles, and is able to uphold ethics within his group. And since both leaders and members often have contradictory principles, a leader should exercise his power to instill his preferred principles to the team.

In summary, leadership has many dimensions. To be an effective decision maker, a leader needs to pay attention to who he is, what he can do, what goals they seek, their honesty, the way they use power, and their values.

Leadership and Collective Purpose

This means that there should be shared decision-making, responsibility, and accountability. In leadership and collective purpose, all members of a business or organization must be involved in building the vision and working together to achieve that vision. This is based on the belief that everyone can and should lead.

Recognizing and Engaging the Strengths of Others

In addition to utilizing own strengths, leaders should also recognize each member's strong points. They should be able to know where members are good and help them improve and learn more. Educators who make a research about organization dynamics and the roles each member has to play in groups often say "people do what they do best." What this means to say is that there are people who every so often become involved and participate positively to the team when they are permitted to do what they are good at and feel comfortable doing them. Members are more confident in groups when they know that they are able to contribute something to the organization coming from their strong points.

Now, the question is, how do leaders determine what their members are good at? There are those who freely express and speak of their strengths. If you find them, they are your people. Obviously, there are times when members would directly and honestly notify their leaders of their strong points. When this happens, leaders should take the time to acknowledge his members' strengths and appoint them to tasks that would capitalize on said strong points.

While it is easy to identify employees' strengths, it is not unusual for leaders to miss out on those. Most of the time, these strong and power points are not visible to leaders or even to member's followers. This makes it challenging because leaders has to determine followers' strengths based on their observations instead of what their followers openly express to them.

Take for instance a member of a group who was just is plodding along, uncertain about her directions and goals. The moment she received a recognition on a challenging task, she became all the more excited and motivated, and was surprised to learn that she has strengths that could benefit the company. Or consider another member, who is never absent, excels at what he does, and never in disagreement of anything. He is pleasing to work with and whose strong points are kindness, considerable, and fun to be with. In these examples, an efficient leader attempts to unfold and recognize members' strengths, and then be able to include them in making the team well-organized and more productive.

Take note though that strengths may not always be openly identifiable. Members of a group or organization may have strengths that are not recognizable or visible because their current state doesn't permit them to showcase such strengths. Therefore, it is important to find opportunities outside followers' normal field of activities that will showcase their strengths.

For example, Madison works as a clerk at a train station. She mainly assists passengers in ticket purchases. The job is very structured and monotonous. Just like her fellow clerks, they all spend most of their working hours inside their assigned cubicle with very few interactions. But there is this one day when Madison's supervisor asked her to organize an event for their company's annual get-together. She now have the opportunity to arrange practices, organize team members and leaders, and promote and write for the company newspaper for the upcoming big event. Thanks to Madison's manager, all these things have been possible.

As a result, many of Madison's' coworkers have noticed her strength when it comes to organizing an event, in communication, and even in writing. All these are not really visible and evident through her day to day clerk duties.

We all know that high-performing teams and groups possess strengths in four areas: relationship building, performing, inspiring, and tactical thinking. When leaders become mindful of their employees' assets, it is easy to assign them to tasks that would challenge their craft and allow them to shine.

Getting to know your members' unique strengths lets leaders assign tasks that will maximize each individual's contribution to the collective goals of the group. If a leader has the ability to effectively execute tasks and have ideas and concepts come into fruition, but does not have a strong point when it comes to building relationships, then the leader should identify members possessing that particular strength. Or, if a leader is good at taking command and connecting with members, he can easily recognize others who are strong in tactical planning and execution. The understanding and knowing of your members' strengths is considered a valuable means to help leaders build effective groups.

In order to practice strength-based leadership, it is important to promote a positive work environment where members' strengths play an important role. There have been studies that state that companies and organizations who are able to create a positive work environment yields a positive physical effect on its members. As an end result, members' performance at work are also improved.

Likewise, there are also employees who become more loyal to the company and do well in their jobs when they are given the chance to show their strengths and use them. Succinct to say, members of any group or organization work effectively when they are in a positive environment.

Leaders who desire to bring about a positive work environment must have these four concepts in mind: communication, relationships, environment, and meaning. In order to foster a positive environment, leaders should promote among their employees virtues such as gratitude, kindness, sympathy, and understanding. Once these are all exhibited, members will feel more confident and productive. Leaders can also promote celebrating people's strengths. This allows for the feeling of being appreciated and respected for their positive contributions and involvement to the team.

In order to develop positive relationships, leaders should reiterate individuals' strengths and positive images instead of their negative images and weaknesses. Recognizing and developing people's greatest assets urge others to do the same thing, and this produces a kind of working environment where everyone is at peace with one another and relationships are far better than those who don't exercise such principle.

In order to develop constructive communication, leaders should make more positive statements than negatives, and evaluate others less negatively. Positive communication helps people feel connected and encourages them to capitalize on their strengths. Finally, leaders can promote positivity in their group by stressing on the relationship between members' morals and ethics and the long-term effect of their jobs. Members of any organization who find sense in what they're doing are more encouraged and productive. This makes the shared goal more achievable and effective.

Teaching Leadership or Manipulation

Manipulation is a kind of act where someone is influenced by a particular deed or belief, only that the manipulator is the one who only gains from one's actions. Leadership, in contrast, ensures that all concerned parties will benefit from the leader's actions. There are leaders who manipulate, but fortunately, there are still those who are fair and just.

The following are some situations that leaders may choose to lead or manipulate. One example is complaining members. Complaining is an aspect that always comes with the territory with workspaces. There are always going to be complainers who are loud and obnoxious in the workplace.

What's a leader to do? You either learn to just deal with them or do something about it. However, one of the best ways to deal with them is to talk to them. If you have people who are complaining, even if you know their constant negativity will somehow affect you and the rest of the members, it is still important that you talk to the person involved, who is active in complaining within a situation. If it is a valid complaint then it is best to talk privately to address the situation.

There are times when given said situation, leaders who are manipulative would just fire said employee. But, an effective leader would sit first and talk to the person or people concerned.

Another situation where you can practice being manipulative or a true leader is office gossips. Gossiping in the office with other coworkers is usually counterproductive and creates an atmosphere of hostility and discomfort for everyone. If your employee has a valid complaint, let him/her voice it. You don't allow that employee to further spread gossip with colleagues and talk about the issue negatively. Instead, be proactive in doing something about it. This action shows initiative and responsibility, which are necessary to accomplish new things in different environments.

If you overhear someone who is complaining and you have to deal with it directly, it's best to just change the subject and talk about something else that is more productive and positive. Also, keeping a positive tone is going to help others experience more joy in their lives. When you can give a positive spin to something, then you can help others to see life on the brighter side, and you can transform your environment into a positive one.

On Creating a Positive Atmosphere in the Workplace

This brings us to our next point: how to create a positive atmosphere? The way to create a positive environment is to be positive yourself. When you are confronted with a negative situation, you should counter it with a positive one. Take for instance, when a person comes to you and says, "See that bunch of good for nothing were causing so much of a stir at the meeting. They were telling everyone how badly they did on the recent collaborative assignment. I hate them. They're always negative."

You can counter this with a positive note like: "Jean, I totally understand the hate and the feeling is draining, but you should understand how frustrated they were feeling. I bet they were having a bad day that's why they did what they did."

What you did there was that you created an environment of empathy for this person. You realized that your member Jean was complaining against a group of people. However, you were seeing things from the other group's perspective and empathized. Also, you told her not to judge them. So, you were effectively negating the negativity of your colleague and making it into a positive one. You could say to Jean, "We all have badly days, and this is probably one of these days for them. Let it slide. Everything's going to turn out well. We have to understand each other and forgive others."

Positivity involves emotional empathy and understanding, but it also consists of looking on the bright side of things so that you can get things done more effectively. Having a positive, upbeat personality is going to enable you to be a great changer in your workplace because you can create that positive vibe that others will experience, and they will want to be around you more because you infuse the atmosphere with positivity. That will also be a motivating factor in getting your colleagues to produce genuinely wonderful work. It will make your colleagues want to go to work and do all the things that they have to do.

You should realize that you have more control in the kind of environment that you're creating with a positive or negative attitude. If you are always positive, you will undoubtedly cause others to feel the same way.

When you are encouraging, you can build others up, and it will create a fantastic environment for you and your colleagues at the workplace. That said, if you are negative all the time, it will bring others down and build a stressed and depressed working environment, which will cause others to suffer and may make you feel better, but at the expense of others.

Negativity, while also powerful, cannot win in the end, because positive feelings are so infectious that they light up a whole office space. When everyone is happy, the entire office is, and the people are prosperous in their work. Moreover, the entire company will be able to produce fantastic work that pays well.

Managers will pay their employees what they're worth, and workers will do their jobs well without any manipulative behavior surfacing. In addition, everyone will be positive because things are going well.

On Providing Appropriate Leadership

In valuing leadership than manipulation at the workplace, it is a great thing to be relational and emotionally aware of what someone is going through in a work placement adjustment. Say, you are a manager, and you have someone who is new to the company for the first time. His name is Christian, and he is quite nervous and unsure of what he is doing. He doesn't know all the rules and has to learn everything from scratch. However, you are there with him to oversee his progress and how he works.

Because you have the empathy to understand where he is coming from and you believe that with proper guidance, you will be able to unleash his skills, you're there to support him. Using your emotional intelligence and experience as a leader, you can effectively guide him in the direction he needs to go. When you see that he is down on his luck for doing something wrong, you can say, "That's definitely fine for a first timer. There's always a next time to do well". You have to be encouraging and provide the guidance that will help him to get back up and keep going.

Emotional intelligence is going to help you relate to your subordinates and colleagues and enable you to connect to others around you, which will help you to be a better leader. When you can see where others have been and are aware that you had been in the same situation, for example, as an intern or as an administrative assistant, then you will be able to empathize with them and provide them with the right kind of guidance, and assist them emotionally and professionally. This will significantly improve your working relationships with others as well.

When to Get Mad and When Not To?

Being emotionally sensitive is going to help you avoid getting too angry at work and will help you to do well at managing others and be a better leader. When you know how to control your emotions, you can do your best to help others achieve their goals. If you don't have enough emotional control, then you will not know how to manage others, and they will resent or hate you for it. You will be the target of your subordinates' judgment and mockery. Therefore, exercising self-control will be crucial in this matter. If you are angry, you should be in a situation where there is a legitimate reason to be angry.

For example, if you find that your subordinates are cheating on their timesheet or if they are doing a sloppy job or taking too long breaks, you should confront them about it and express your displeasure with what they are doing. What they're doing deserves disciplinary action. It is crucial that you find ways of getting your colleague's attention in a way that lets them know that what they are doing is wrong and needs to be done away with.

On the other hand, getting angry with someone for no reason can cause rifts in relationships and problems at the office. Thus, it is vital that you get your act together and not get angry at smaller things that don't matter. Instead, let the petty stuff go. This will make things a lot better for you and your colleagues at work.

Chapter 4 – Emotional Intelligence

Introduction

Most people tend to describe good or bad emotions. So, love, excitement, and happiness are' good' emotions, and' bad' emotions are anxiety, sadness, and anger. Nevertheless, if some emotions are characterized as' evil,' you are likely to be even more negative. For example, for several people, it is relatively common to feel depressed and culpable as they say to themselves, "Why should you feel depressed when you have a stable career? A good job, financially secure, and your children are doing well?" By defining depression as' bad?' The person now feels both depressed and guilty in this case! Okay, depression is already disagreeable enough, and effort is needed to resolve, why judge your emotions and add another frustrating emotion? Never judge your emotions to regain control of your feelings! Psychologists will ask you to look at every emotion as pleasant, but either nice or disagreeable.

To be emotionally intelligent is to be able to understand your emotional states of being conscious. Feeling' emotional' means that you are conscious of the sensation of being. Being "smart" means you have reasonable knowledge or a logical understanding of the current situation, occurrence, and circumstances. You are smart if you can rationalize consciously what is happening in your life. You become emotional when you can sense your body-emotional self-awareness.

What Is Emotional Intelligence and How Does It Impact the Workplace?

You have heard about emotional quotient, EQ, and emotional intelligence before, almost certainly, but have you ever wondered if you are emotionally intelligent? Were you emotionally intelligent at work to go a step further? As a leader, what about it? You might have asked yourself why emotional intelligence is so critical if you have considered these questions. Emotional intelligence will be explored in this book and its relevance for every individual, every workplace, every society, and even the whole world.

What is emotional intelligence?

Emotional intelligence is the capacity to interpret emotions, to access emotions, to produce emotions, to understand emotions and emotional information, and to reflectively control emotions to promote emotional and intellectual growth.

Standardized tests assess emotional intelligence, and the outcome is Emotional Quotient (EQ). The higher the EQ, the better. Nevertheless, as opposed to the Intelligence Quotient (IQ), mostly calculated when you reach a certain age, most researchers and psychologists agree that EQ is malleable, strengthened, and trained.

Why does emotional intelligence matter?

EQ may not be so known as IQ, but many experts find it more relevant than IQ. Why? Why? Studies show that EQ is a better predictor of a person's success, relationship quality, and happiness. It is apparent and essential in all aspects of life. You've ever heard someone saying: "Wow, what a good person! He's going to achieve a great thing in life certainly," or' She's very caring and sociable. She's so great boss.' These comments show that if a person has high EQ (even if the person doesn't know that), others can see and feel it. It is these types of people that others most likely believe would thrive. What, then, is EQ essential to all?

1. EQ is an essential element in the formation, development, maintenance, and enhancement of personal relationships with others. It is undeniable that it is most likely that people who know how to build positive relations with others will succeed in their fields. High EQ workers can work in teams harmoniously and adapt to changes. No matter how intelligent you are, you may find the path to success if you have low emotional intelligence. There's good news, though. Take comfort in knowing that, at any age and regardless of past actions, you will develop your EQ skills.

2. To be aware implies to be able to deal with constructive criticism. You probably agree that there is no perfect person in the world and that you need feedback and encouragement from others to do better in everything you do. You are self-conscious, if you have a high EQ, to understand your strengths, to admit your shortcomings, and to

understand how your behaviors affect other people around you. Your high EQ enables you to use these critiques to improve your performance. This is a crucial part of working with many stakeholders in an environment.

3. Self-motivated people will empower everything. If a person is motivated by himself, others around him also assess their motivation. A self-motivated person is confident and guided by what matters to him/her. Who wouldn't want a person with self-motivation, right? Motivation is infectious, and a family, workplace, or community with high motivation can consistently outperform unmotivated ones. Low motivation may be a sign that in one or more major EQ quadrants, the emotional quotient is low.

4. EQ is true to the world. People with a high emotional quotient have compassion that helps them to respond to others at an "emotional" level. If a person can sympathize with others, he/she can work sincerely and listen to the needs of others with compassion and concern—even during difficult times.

5. A high EQ means that you can control yourself in all circumstances. Your friend yells loudly at you for some unknown reason. Given this scenario, could you control your emotions and not do the same thing? You see, EQ is linked to how both your positive and your negative emotions are managed. Think of some of the decisions you're not proud of in your life. Ask yourself how many of them have to do with the lack of self-control or impulse control? The response might be incredible.

Were you sure about what emotional intelligence and moral quotient were? Would you accept that it is more important than being "book-smart?" Do you understand why EQ is the key to success? The task is to recognize when emotional intelligence is lacking. It is often clear that there is a problem, but what the problem is exactly can be a mystery.

Here's a challenge for you as you know what you know about emotional intelligence. Ask yourself this question: are you at home and work an emotionally intelligent person? If it is yes, then you're on the right path! Continue this path, improve your EQ skills as you advance, and you could be productive. Don't stress if your answer is no. Emotional intelligence is a collection of skill that can be enhanced by concentration and a sound strategy. No matter where you are today, believing in yourself and developing your emotional intelligence skills cannot be incorrect.

The Importance of Having an Emotionally Intelligent Workforce

Emotional awareness. The term continued to appear everywhere at the moment was even mentioned in relation to Big Brother on the Ryan Tubridy breakfast this morning! What is so essential about emotional intelligence or E.I., and how important does it matter to you as a person in your life, job, training, and development?

What is Quality determining?

In 1905, Alfred Binet administered the first French cognitive intelligence test. This was later renamed the Stanford-Binet test after it had been standardized for the American population at Stanford University. Since then, many have argued that only one of our intelligence (other emotional, spatial, musical, and artistic) was assessed during the study. It took more than 50 years to take Emotional Intelligence seriously. Emotional intelligence is how you interact with yourself, with other people, and with life in general. It's characterized as a set of non-cognitive capabilities, competencies, and skills that influence the ability to cope with environmental requirements and stresses, and that is a factor in determining one's ability to succeed in life. The average student often saw the high-performers at school as good. However, proof does not prove that this is the case. Studies were conducted following children from primary, secondary, and third-level schooling. We then went to these same individuals in various stages to test how we lived in the race called life and took on all facets, including work, home, and the family. What they found was that academic success is not always "good." The average student was often the most successful if all aspects of his / her life were taken into account, often with better work and happy homes. The only factor in determining success is cognitive intelligence or IQ; another intelligence is at work, which is emotional intelligence.

Unpredictable behaviour

Did you ever work in an environment which the atmosphere was tense, because of one member's erratic behavior? Do you remember (or experience) the stress caused by such an atmosphere? Have you ever noticed the domino effect on everybody at work? How can you work appropriately in such an atmosphere if you anticipate a sudden outburst of uncontrolled anger, verbal abuse, blame or criticism, sudden high or lower moods? This is not the right way of working, nor is it a positive way of working. If this person is a supervisor or manager, it is particularly stressful.

People work best and are much more efficient and productive in a happy and relaxed environment. We want to go to work and work more effectively; we are also able to do so. So how do you enhance your actions, your working environment, and all the interconnected areas? The solution is the application of emotional intelligence.

The Use of Emotional Intelligence

Emotional Intelligence: Why it can matter more than IQ (1995), the use of emotional intelligence. Emotional Intelligence is "Ability to consider our own and others ' feelings, empower ourselves, to handle emotions well in ourselves and our relationships." This ability was not exercised by the volatile workplace member mentioned above, and his colleagues thus suffered as a result. The emotional capacity was unavailable, and the skills needed to cope with everyday life and work pressure (as described by Dr. Bar-on) were not established. His colleagues suffered due to this individual's lack of emotional intelligence. For teams and companies in general, emotional intelligence can also be missing. The good news is that if areas of weakness are found, they can be worked on and strengthened in a person, team, or company.

Many are concerned with the increasing awareness of E.I. In 1990. "the ability to monitor your feelings and emotions, to differentiate between you and to use this knowledge to direct your thoughts and actions," is a term that is highly relevant to behavior within the working environment and would create an emotionally intelligent atmosphere where an unpredictable behavior described above would be generated.

If the E.I., there will be no real impact on training and development, education, or team building. It is underdeveloped by the individual or group: introduction and use of E.I. The quality of the workplace, in general, can be improved in corporate environments, irrespective of business operation, or scale. E.I. E.I. It is essential at all levels and if E.I is adopted and implemented by higher levels. This will filter down through a company in their daily dealings with all peers and employees.

Where emotional intelligence can be assessed, and the term Emotional Quotient or EQ established, which in turn leads to EQ-I ® or Emotional-quotient inventories ®. The psychometric test is the most accepted E.I measure. Available. Available. It measures E.I. It measures centered on five scales further divided into 15 subscales. The results of the inventory show how effective you are, as individuals and as teams.

The EQ-I ® scales are:

- Intrapersonal — assess our awareness and control of one's own emotions.
- Interpersonal–tests our capacity to communicate with others and to get along.
- Adaptability-measures how versatile you are and your problem-solving ability.
- Stress management-measures the amount of stress you tolerate and control your impulses.
- General Mood-measures our satisfaction and motivation

The areas evaluated in the EQ-I ® relate to a team as well as the participant. If a team is to work well and improve its efficiency, it must be conscious of its IT; greater cooperation, innovation, and productivity will result. E.I. is a squad. The EI of the individual members is not measured, but the E.I calculate. A synergistic relationship between the whole group.

In an organization, emotional intelligence can be implemented in different ways. It begins as a new employee joins a business. This explores how workers relate to each other, how managers manage, how an organization, and many other things, respond to the needs of its people.

E.I. I. Based training and development will concentrate on relevant skills, including interpersonal relations, stress management, problem-solving, and leadership skills. Where vulnerability areas are tested in advance using the EQ-I ® test–test choices include a leadership survey, a group/team report, and a personal report–outcomes of EI-based training are improved.

What Being Emotionally Intelligent Does Not Mean

A person with emotional intelligence was identified as the one who has found the most effective way to CONTROL and to use his / her emotions to improve performance and learning. Of the above, one can correctly infer that the ability to CONTROL and use one's emotions to change those goals is what makes a person qualified as emotionally intelligent.

The number of the main attributes/qualities usually shown by an emotionally intelligent person as

1. Capacity to inspire him/her to reach a specific goal(s).2. The ability to persevere despite frustration adversity i.e., things go badly.

3. The ability to control desires and defer gratification ensures that immediate pleasure is delayed in order to ensure the long-term goal of financial security, for example.

4. Mental strength is shown by the ability to regulate one's moods and prevent swamping one's ability to think.

5. The capacity for empathy i.e., attention to others ' feelings or emotions.

6. The ability to keep up with other people.

7. Capacity to reach "flow" or "path."

Emotionally intelligent people are the ones needed to succeed an entrepreneur. A careful look at the lives/stories of many successful business people shows that they have met their goals by demonstrating the qualities of Emotionally Smart.

The above explains why - and Why-most of today's highly successful businessmen are dropping out in many parts of the world (or, in some instances, just UN-schooled). This also shows that the lack of formal schooling is NOT a fatal barrier to life success.

Emotional Intelligence Can be taught. It is generally recognized that the most important emotional skills can be learned and developed- especially from childhood—unlike IQ, which can not be modified much by education.

Academic intelligence, as this book states, offers virtually no preparation for the nuances of adversity or the opportunities life experiences bring.

But what emotional intelligence is NOT. There is a problem in the way some people quickly label the claim that intellectual ability / IQ is not guarantee of success in life. They pronounce "being together" loudly as a critical skill / emotional competence that is essential to social progress.

While it is understood that "interpersonal talent" is indeed an essential skill, my remarks of some who highlight this "going together with others" for success, make me nervous that they believe it must be achieved at all costs.

In other words, the INTEGRITY and SINCERITY of intent/purpose are NOT taken into account.

Now the most significant risk of such reasoning is that it unwittingly gives a vest of legitimacy to insincere and deceptive people who use their social relationships for egotistical purposes. (For example, to look good or to obtain broad approval from everybody they think is necessary or relevant).

When' getting along with others' does not translate into being emotionally intelligent in the TRUE sense, it is essential to identify specific instances.

This term describes certain people in society who are (as he puts it)' champions of making good impressions. They're usually led by a NEED to curry favor, to win acceptance from others almost at any cost-a a negative form of' getting along with others,' I believe.

Chapter 5 - Emotional Leadership

Emotional Leader Definition

To become an effective leader, one must show emotional intelligence. Although this concept only emerged years ago, it has attracted the interests of many scholars and practitioners of leadership. Emotional intelligence is aimed at understanding other people's emotions and then applying them to everyday work experiences.

To define, emotional intelligence is a leader's capacity to express and identify feelings, utilize these emotions to enable appropriate thinking, be able to comprehend and make proper reasoning, and control and handle it with ease especially within the workplace.

The underlying premise of research on emotional intelligence is that people who are sensitive to their own emotions and the impact their emotions have on others will be more effective leaders.

Since showing emotional intelligence is positively related to effective leadership, what should a leader do to enhance his or her emotional skills?

First, a leader needs to constantly assess how he or she is feeling and what's causing those feelings no matter how good or bad he feels.

Second, a leader should be trained in being sensitive to other's feelings. A leader who knows how to read others' emotions is better equipped to respond appropriately to people's wants and needs. Stated another way, a leader needs to have empathy for others. He or she should understand the feelings of others as if those feelings were his or her own. Empathy is the critical component of emotional intelligence.

Third, a leader has to learn how to control his emotions. Whenever he makes a big decision, the leader's emotions are involved. Therefore, emotions need to be embraced and managed for the good of the group or organization. When a leader knows how to appropriately manage his emotions, he increases the chances that the group's decisions will be effective.

For example, a school directress sensed that she was becoming extremely angry with some students who pulled a prank during an assembly. Instead of being extremely angry for ruining the assembly, she chose to maintain her demeanor and helped to turn the prank into a learning experience. The key point here is that people who are emotionally intelligent recognize different emotions, include take note of, and include them in what they do as leaders.

An emotionally intelligent leader listens to his feelings and that of others. He is also adept at regulating these emotions in service of the common good.

Leaders must control their emotions alone and have to have a high degree of self-control to function as productive individuals in a business or company. In particular, a leader must deal with the negative emotions that can easily overwhelm and discourage, including anger, anxiety, and frustration, to prevent any negative responses that can result in regrettable behavior.

Self-regulation enables a leader to recognize the stimuli that are causing a person to act out on their emotions, keep them in check, and respond in appropriate ways that will help them in a given situation.

There are different techniques that a person can practice, to improve in this area of emotional wellness. That includes meditation, mindfulness, and other ways of managing stress. With emotional leadership, a leader learns how to reduce the intensity of the experience of emotions. For example, an angry leader can think of happy thoughts or amusing things that will help him laugh off the situation.

Regulating one's emotions involve an element of distracting the person from the situation to cope in response to said situation. It is also known as "down-regulation," which is useful for playing down the emotions to calm and soothe a person into responding in appropriate and constructive ways.

To get a fuller grasp of the kind of training it might be like, we must take note in great detail some of the methods in which intelligence can be brought to our emotions. This may not be new, but in recent years, they have attempted to bring emotions in the area of intellect, instead of seeing intellect and emotion in disagreement in terms.

Other psychologists took a more pessimistic view of social intelligence, seeing it in terms of skills that manipulate others or the means to get people to do what you tell them to do, whether they approve of it or not. But none of these held much power and influence with logicians of IQ.

However, personal intelligence should not be ignored, mainly because it makes both intuitive and common sense.

Emotional intelligence has 4 basic domains:

1. Knowing one's emotions. The awareness of one's feelings is considered a keystone of emotional intelligence. The capacity of a leader to monitor his feelings from time to time is considered important to self-understanding. People who are well aware of their feelings and emotions are considered better navigators of their lives. This is because they are certain of how they would feel given the

chance to decide on important matters whether it be personal or career wise.

2. Managing emotions. This is another important factor as it helps examine a leader's power to soothe oneself, eliminate rampant irritability and even anxiety, and the consequences of failure. Those leaders who lack the ability to manage their emotions always have issues with their feelings of distress. On the other hand, those who are good at this can easily recover more quickly from life's challenges and hurts.

3. Motivating oneself. To motivate oneself, a leader must know how to martial his emotions for a specific goal. Self-control and delaying gratification motivate accomplishment. And, a leader who is able to go into the flow allows for an outstanding performance of all sorts. Leaders who particularly possess this kind of skill is definitely more effective and productive in whatever they do.

4. Recognizing emotions in others. This is often called as empathy or the capacity of a person to have emotional self-awareness. If you are an empathic person, it simply means that you are more in agreement to the subtle signs specifying what others want or need. This makes for an empathic and effective leader.

What is Emotional Intelligence in Leadership?

Emotional intelligence in leadership can enhance your emotional sensitivity to help you have success in the workplace. We know that you want to get ahead where you work, and we want to give you the tools to do that. So, we are going to provide you with a step-by-step guide to raise your emotional intelligence (EQ) and give you the right tools to enable you to be successful in your goals and aspirations.

Let's start with the emotions themselves. Begin with the basic emotions, and then you can move on to the more subtle and advanced emotions as you go along. Throughout your journey, we advise you to keep a journal of your thoughts to record how you're doing with it.

At the beginning of this journey to emotional understanding, we should start with how you experience emotions and your way of recognizing them. You have to become self-aware and examine how you are experiencing emotions from day to day. It all begins with self-regulation of the emotions.

One way to be self-aware is to write down your thoughts and experiences from day to day. Get a journal and start writing down especially the ones that are causing you stress or anxiety. You should learn how to recognize when you are feeling angry or sad, and take note of what you think triggered or caused this negative emotion to come about.

You should think about how you are reacting to each situation. For example, if you were angry, perhaps you became enraged and started shouting or throwing things. Alternatively, if you were sad or depressed, you went to your room and cried it out.

Once you have gauged how you responded to each situation, then you can evaluate how you responded to the scenario. Think to yourself: "was this an appropriate response?" "Is this the right way to respond to the situation?" "Did I overreact?"

Or, perhaps, you experienced a positive emotion that helped to solve a situation. For example, maybe you were able to solve a problem yourself that you thought was really difficult, then you discovered there was a simple solution and could laugh it off and think that it was no big deal. Often, we can learn to laugh at ourselves; it can help lessen the pressure we always out on ourselves and feel more peaceful.

To fully understand how emotional regulation works, we have to look at some concrete examples of self-awareness.

The usefulness of emotional intelligence is a comparatively a new concept for business, and some leaders find it difficult to acknowledge. Some of them are a little apprehensive because empathy would somehow place them in conflicting interests with regards to their administrative objectives. One felt the idea of sensing the feelings of those who worked for him was absurd. Others protested that if they were not emotionally aloof, they would be unable to make the hard decisions that the business requires—although the possibility is that they bring forth and come up with more compassionate decisions.

Relationship-oriented leaders often look at the significance in being instead of doing. So rather than focusing on tasks, emotional leaders who have high emotional intelligence are more concerned with connecting with others. They are fond of celebrating relationships as well as the delight that come with it.

Furthermore, relationship-oriented leaders often have a strong orientation in the present. They always value being in the moment. In a group situation, sensing and feeling the company of others is appealing to these people. They have been described as relationship junkies. Basically, these people are into connectedness.

In a work setting, the relationship-oriented leader wants to connect or attach with others. For example, they would not be afraid to interrupt someone who is working hard on a task to talk about the weather, sports, or just about anything. When solving an issue, these people like to talk and address the matter immediately. They fins satisfaction just by being connected to others.

A task-oriented person described a relationship-oriented person perfectly when he said, "He is the kind of person who talks to you, coffee mug in hand, when you're trying to do an important task such as beating a deadline or writing a book." The sense in "doing" is just not dominant in the style of the relationship-oriented person.

Good leaders understand the work that needs to be done, as well as the need to understand the people who will do it. This process necessitates that leaders pay attention to both tasks and relationships. The challenge here is to determine how much task and how much relationship is required in a given situation or context.

Emotional leadership helps members feel at ease with themselves, with one other, and with the situation in which they find themselves. For example, in the classroom, when a teacher requires each student to know every other student's name, the teacher is demonstrating emotional leadership. The teacher is helping students to feel comfortable with themselves, with other students, and with their environment.

Researchers have described emotional leadership in several ways that help to clarify its meaning. It has been labeled by some researchers as consideration behavior, which consists of solidarity, trust, and showing respect to both regard between leaders and members. Other researchers describe this kind of leadership as having an employee orientation, which encompasses showing interest towards coworkers, valuing their individuality, and providing consideration to their individual needs. Another line of research has simply defined leadership as being concerned with people.

In a company, showing concern and affection to members encompasses building good working conditions, trust, maintaining a fair structure, and promoting good social relations.

In essence, when you use emotional intelligence in leadership, it all boils down into these: treat others with dignity and respect, help people whenever possible, get along well with others, and create an amiable work setting. In order to foster effective leadership, one must make emotional intelligence an essential part of it.

In this diverse and fast-paced society, a leader's major challenge is to find the energy and time to listen to members and do what is required in order to create good relationship among each other.

For those who are highly relationship-oriented in their personal lives, being emotionally intelligent in leadership will come easily. For those who value tasks more than anything else, being relationship-oriented in leadership will present a greater challenge. Regardless of your leadership styles, every leadership situation demands a degree of emotional leadership behavior.

Task and relationship leadership are connected with each other, and one of the challenges is to incorporate these two in the best possible way, and at the same time, effectively familiarizing to your members' needs.

For instance, task leadership is salient when you are dealing with a large number of newly hired employees. In a situation like this, members feel unsure about their responsibilities, and they would appreciate having a leader that would clarify things and let them know what exactly is expected of them. In fact, in nearly every group or situation, there are some individuals who want and need task direction from their leader, and in these circumstances, it is paramount that the leader exhibit strong task-oriented leadership.

On the other hand, it is also true that there are members who prefer to be connected to the leader rather than they care for direction. For instance, at a workplace, there are employees who would rather have someone call them their friend and be able to connect to them on an equal level.

The members are willing to work, but they are primarily interested in being recognized and feeling related to others. An example would be individuals who attend a cancer support group. They like to receive information from the leader, but even more importantly, they want the leader to relate to them. It is similar with individuals who attend a community-sponsored reading club. They want to talk about the book, but they also want the leader to relate to them in a more familiar way. Clearly, in these situations, the leader needs to connect with followers by utilizing relationship oriented behaviors.

In society, the most effective leaders recognize and adapt to members' needs. Whether they are team leaders, teachers, or managers, they appropriately demonstrate the right degrees of task and relationship leadership. This is no small challenge because different followers and situations demand different amounts of task and relationship leadership. When followers are unclear, confused, or lost, the leader needs to show direction and exhibit task-oriented leadership. At the same time, a leader needs to be able to see the need for affiliation in members and to meet said needs, sans the expense of task completion.

In the end, when you say best leader, it means being able to help members realize work goals by means of getting on with the task at hand and to each member.

We all know leaders who do this: They are leaders who force us to do drills until we are blue in the face to improve our physical performance, but who then caringly listen to our personal issues. They are the managers who never let us slack off for even a second but who make work a fun place to be. The list goes on, but the bottom line is that the best leaders get the job done and care about others in the process.

In conclusion, good leaders are both task oriented and relationship oriented. Taking note of your personal styles in leadership can help you have a better recognition of your leadership. Task-oriented people find meaning in doing, while emotional-oriented people find meaning in being connected to others. Effective leadership requires that leaders be both task oriented and emotional oriented.

Action Steps Emotional Intelligence

Behavior is said to be another area to emotional intelligence. Leaders who are deemed to be emotionally-intelligent are the ones who have the capacity to identify behavioral types. These are leaders who are able to identify their own emotional conditions and that of others. They can easily get along well with others and make use of their emotions as a way to empathize with the members of an organization.

The moment you know and fully grasp different kinds of emotions, you can effectively lead your members and will have a superior control over everything. When you are in control of your emotions, you will be able to master your feelings. It likewise improves your communication skills. Yes, all these go hand in hand. They are akin to a chain reaction. There is a purpose for everything, and that very purpose is to help one another.

Success and happiness are both possible if you learn to value and accept yourself.

These are needed, directly or indirectly, in all elements of emotional intelligence. Beware though because most of the time, people put on a poker face – confident on the outside but full of insecurities on the inside.

There are two ways to check this – If you have a high self-regard, your concern, empathy towards other people will naturally show, and you become fully aware of your strengths and weaknesses. You do not mind hearing criticisms all because you do not see them as threat but as a way to improve yourself.

How about your regard for other people? When you say high regard for others, it means that you value and accept them no matter their status in the society. What this means to say is that even if you don't agree with what they do, you still give your full respect to the person behind those actions – inappropriate or not.

The problem here is a combination of values and emotionally unintelligent behavior. Take for instance, Janet. Honesty is not an important value for her, so her friend's lies do not evoke a strong emotional reaction in her. However, honesty is a core value for Manny, so each time he hears Janet's friend's stories, he reacts strongly. The strong negative emotions Manny feels influences his thinking and results in him making a moral judgement of

Janet as a person and as a friend. What gives Manny the right to judge Janet? How can he brand her as a horrible person? This is because Manny is a kind of person who values the feelings of other people. He is aware that lies could break a person, and both Janet and her friend will not benefit from lies.

Self-awareness is the level by which you are in one with your intuition, feelings, and your body. How does one develop awareness of self? Keep in mind, feelings are a whole body experience. Increasing awareness of both intuition and feelings include learning to adapt and listen to what is going on in our body and how said changes, if there are any, affect our behavior. Likewise, it's amazing how we immediately feel if something does not sit well. This is because the emotional brain communicates through sensations or feelings or experienced by the body. That is what you call intuition.

Since intuition obviously can't speak in words, it has to look for other ways. Some of the signs include headaches, muscle tension, sleepless nights, appetite loss, and butterflies in the stomach among other physical signs. If we listen to our intuition and are in touch with our emotions, it will surely tell you what is right from wrong.

Awareness of Others

Are you concerned of other people's feelings and wellbeing? Do they matter to you? To help enhance awareness of others, you need to learn skills. Take note though that you only get to learn if you have genuine concern for others.

The following are steps to take for emotional intelligence. These are also known as core skills required in order to become effective as a leader.

1. Empathy skills
2. Listening skills
3. Questioning skills

Let's take a careful look at how these three skills can be developed.

1. Empathy skill

This is deemed as the foundation for positive relationships. It hones your ability to respond and recognize other people's feelings, fears, and even their issues in life. When you say empathy, it doesn't necessarily mean that you are judging people based on their actions. Instead, you make a conscious effort to put yourself into their position and point of view. This is how you understand and become more conscious of their feelings.

Failing to be empathic will make communication difficult. You will find it hard to give compliments to others, converse with people, and there will be times when you don't really want to talk with others. This is because you either feel insensitive, you always see the negative traits in others, and you tend to always jump into conclusions.

Developing the empathy skill requires understanding of others and seeing the good side in them.

2. Listening skill

To be more aware of this skill, it is important that you determine the constant barriers. What are the usual incidences that get in the way for you to become an effective listener?

Do you

- Easily get distracted by views and judgments that are more often than not don't have anything to do with the person involved?
- Find yourself always interrupting or butting in when someone's talking? Interrupt the other person?
- Label a person with the way he talks and how he airs his or her opinions?
- Stop listening because you are planning what to say next?
- Based your views about the person on your initial knowledge about him or her?
- Refuse to have eye contact?
- Interrupt someone's train of thought while talking?

Emotional listening requires complete focus and effort on your part. In this skill, you are listening for the tone of voice, emotions, and feelings, and not just mere words. In this level, the receiver is really trying to absorb what the other person is saying.

To improve this kind of skill, the next time you listen to a person talking, keep your mind on the kind of listening you find comfortable to utilize. Do you focus on facts? Do your thoughts begin to wander when somebody talks? Do you easily forget details? Do you focus on emotions? Try to evaluate what you particularly focus on and those that you easily ignore either intentionally or not, and make it a point to improve on those.

3. Questioning skill

This is another skill that helps you understand people. Asking the right questions will aid in easily resolving conflicts, in making other speak their minds, and properly expressing themselves.

The Power of Emotional Intelligence

Attitudes, values, and beliefs all have a commanding connection with a person's feelings, thoughts, and behaviors. Take for instance a tree. Imagine a tree being a representation of who you are, the trunk representing your attitude, and the branches and leaves as your actions and behavior. Attitudes, values, and beliefs are considered the same according to many psychologists. Values are an inherent element of who you are, and these are less variable than that of attitudes and beliefs.

Here's a rundown of each element in detail to help you in becoming the best version of yourself:

Values

It is a gift to know your values because they help shape who you are as a person and provide an explanation as to why you respond or behave the way you do. Have you ever experienced being picked on by someone? You probably either shrugged it off or reacted aggressively. When you are fully aware of your core values, you know the things that matter to you. You know when to react and when to just let things go.

Knowing your values likewise gives you freedom. This is because you know what you really want to do and do it, instead of not doing what you think you should be doing.

Think about what's important in your life. In emotional leadership training, it is always asked what's important to you. While many will answer their family, friends, or career, take note though that these cannot be considered as values. These are just representations. To get beneath the surface of these said priorities, you'll be asked, what does your family, friends, or career give or bring to you? If we are to take the example of family, some people would answer, the feeling of belongingness and being loved. So, if your family is what matters to you, what is it that they bring or give you?

Getting deeper into your values and understanding takes coaching and mentoring to fully comprehend them. In order to access your emotional brain, a coach will have to ask you the above-mentioned questions instead of sticking to logical questions.

The Impact of Values

Let us consider first your values' impact being uncoordinated. Take for instance, if someone or a situation is stepping into your values, what impact does it have on you?

Knowing your values means having high regard for others. You are especially respectful of each other's differences. And if your values are not balanced, you are likely to take action such as being more self-aware. Just like in the example above, you may choose to just shrug the situation off or react violently. However, if you values are in line, you would most definitely choose the former and let it pass. This is easier to do when your values are in line. However, if it is the other way around, you will feel more stressed out, discontent, and in extreme.

Values in Leadership

Values are an essential part of leadership. Let's take for instance the perspective of the leader and followers. In the previous chapters, we have learned that it is important for leaders to develop their emotional intelligence. It is important that you have high self-regard or else, you won't take the necessary measures to ascertain that you're in line with your values. The significance of working from a healthy position as a leader should not be undervalued.

When you are aware of your core values, you are performing from an informed regard of being true and what works for you when leading others.

Another thing to consider is the clash of values. If you think a certain situation will have an impact on your values, you have to carefully consider it. Leaders who have identified their values will help them use them effectively within the working relationship to check on the right course of action.

Just take note that interpretations can be different from person to person. As a leader, it is important that you don't make assumptions about the meaning of a specific member or follower's values.

The Importance of Values at Work

Values are considered the hidden threads between profit, performance, and people. However, there are companies and organizations that got it completely wrong when with comes to what values are all about. How many times have you seen organizations with their values pinned on the office wall? Do employees really know what these company values mean? Do both leaders and followers practice said values? Unfortunately, it is rare.

Aspirational values and stated ones are fine, but what really matters is the experienced and real ones within the company. By tradition, many leaders have stressed the importance of value rather than values. However, when values are used well, it gives them a competitive edge over others.

Remember that values shouldn't be stated alone. They need to be properly understood so that everyone will live to practice said values.

While values determine what drives you, attitudes and beliefs likewise affect one's behavior and the results you gain.

The Link between Beliefs, Values, and Attitude

All three are interconnected with each other in that they all have an impact on one's actions and behavior on a day-to-day basis. Habits are formed through repetition. Therefore, determine what values drive your attitude and beliefs.

With repetition, you form habits. As a leader, your values, attitudes, and beliefs will influence greatly the kind of questions you ask your members. In the same way, a leader's attitudes, beliefs, and values will impact how your members will react and respond to questions as well as the actions they will take. This is because leaders have the power to influence and shift limiting values, beliefs, and attitudes to help their members think outside the box.

Attitudes and Values in EI Context

Your attitudes and values reside in your emotional brain and are considered a strong force in your life. They affect your manners and actions, which eventually influence the outcome and performance in life.

Recognizing and valuing your own and others' values is salient in self-regard and regard for others. It is by keeping up with high self-awareness that you'll determine if your values are being walked on and you can utilize self-management to return them back to their place. Conversely, high regard to the feeling of others enables you to be respectful of them and know if you are already stepping into the line. An Emotionally Intelligent leader are highly conscious of their beliefs, attitudes, and values that influences their leading and managing ability.

The Emotionally Intelligent Company or Organization

A company or organization that practices this has the power to recognize that everyone has a unique set of beliefs, values, and attitudes. When hiring a new staff, the company will see if the values the company upholds match with the person's values as well. Remember, it is easier to train skills, but very challenging to train values, and sometimes this isn't possible.

It also upholds company values that will be carried out by its leaders and members. They will be aligned with positive behaviors and attitudes that everyone will be familiar with. The members will be more aware of what's expected of them and how their roles will fit in with the company's set of values.

Take for instance a telecommunication company that went through a process of recognizing company values. It classified leaders and decision makers along with employees in outlining core values. To help everyone understand, it was broken down into these:

Respect, Values, Attitude: We respect ourselves and our coworkers, as well as our clients.

Behaviors: We take high regard for our service and our word. Should we think we will fail to deliver, we'll keep you informed as soon as possible.

Everyone must be completely aligned with the company's values with all best interests always in mind.

In order to implement and define values, here are 5 steps in a company setting that should be understood and lived by everyone involved:

Step 1. Define the values with the team, and if possible, a cross-section of employees.

Step 2. Describe the meaning of said values. Appropriate interpretation matters.

Step 3. Label the type of attitudes you require in the organization that are in line with the values. Remember that these values should be applied to everyone.

Step 4. Define behaviors linked to these attitudes and values. List sets of behaviors that are linked to each value.

Step 5. Communicate behaviors through meetings and be innovative and resourceful on how you distribute and use them for everyone to read and learn.

If you are a leader, you need to walk the talk. Values should not only be stated, but should be experienced and lived. Use the company values as benchmark in recruiting and leading your members. Also, make it a point that these values are visible in the company premises for everyone to be reminded and actually live them.

How Emotional Intelligence Can Really Help Out in Relationships

One of the most crucial parts of emotional intelligence is how you recognize and differentiate negative emotions. We must see that it is normal to feel one way and we shouldn't make a moral judgment against the negative emotions as if it is terrible to experience such things. Sometimes, our emotions are triggered by a sense of justice, and when we see unjust actions and behaviors, we want justice served.

For example, if you get angry at how a person is being treated at the workplace, you have the right to get mad about it. A sense of justice can produce a kind of "righteous" anger in that you may realize that something is wrong, and you want to correct it. However, what you do with this emotion matters.

Emotional intelligence at work is going to help you to put all your emotions in check. You'll have to go through the process of getting your feelings in check. Furthermore, there is a step-by-step process to get there.

The following are some of benefits of emotional intelligence in all aspects of life, whether at work or in personal relationships:

1. *You're always optimistic*

Emotional intelligence helps you have a positive outlook in people and in life in general. It helps you to become positive all the time. You should enjoy the beautiful emotions that you have and not dwell on the negative thoughts that you might experience.

Let yourself smile and laugh even at difficult things. You should also learn to laugh at yourself whenever you make mistakes because everyone is prone to making an error, and that's part of being human.

To leverage your positive emotions, you need to find the time to enjoy positivity and surround yourself with others who will do the same. Try to counter all the negative thoughts you may be experiencing with positive ones. It will make a difference, and you will notice how you come across to others.

Many leaders are quite critical of their members and don't hesitate to point out all the mistakes in their employees' record of work. They tend to dwell on giving negative feedback to others, and this causes a significant amount of problems, because the workers may feel fearful or worried about their performance as a result of mistakes they have made.

If a leader lashes out in anger, then this will impact the motivation of the worker and may lead to employee dissatisfaction and discouragement. Therefore, as a leader, you need to find ways to look at the brighter side of things and learn to control your negative response. By being positive and exuding that positivity, you can make a difference in transforming the work culture of your company. It will make for happy workers and leaders.

2. *Describe and Understand Your Emotions*

Being able to label your emotions and understand what it is that you are feeling is another benefit. This is a technique used in talk therapy such as cognitive behavioral therapy or dialectical behavioral therapy for people dealing with various mental health challenges. Primary emotions are the body's way of reacting to triggers that might cause a person stress. For example, if you see someone being mistreated at work and they are getting criticized by the higher ups, you have the right to feel angry about it. You can identify what it is that is triggering the negative emotion in you: injustice and think about ways you can deal with that emotion.

How do you label and understand an emotion? When you start feeling an emotion, you talk about what it is. When you begin to feel depressed, you can tell yourself, "I think I'm starting to feel down today. Maybe I should go for a walk or run and get those endorphins flowing again." Alternatively, when you're starting to feel stressed out about something, you can start telling yourself, "I'm feeling nervous, and in order to remove stress, I need to get this project done."

Identifying the emotion is an essential step because once you know exactly what it is that you are feeling and why you can come up with ways to manage the symptoms of what you're feeling, it is easier to deal with them. You can formulate the most positive responses to almost all kinds of negative situations.

3. *Allows You to Enjoy Life*

Life is too short to be all serious and stressed out. As a leader, it is important that you have a positive work-life balance and encourage your employees to do the same. The best thing about emotional intelligence in leadership is that you develop empathy around you. You understand their feelings and their situation that you wish they have an enjoyable life as well.

Enjoying life encourages you to be balanced, and you can also model that to your employees. By leading a balanced life and finding room for work and play, you will also help in regulating your emotions and feel happier in the process.

In addition, you should also foster this spirit of fun by inviting your colleagues and subordinates to a company get together every once in a while. With the social aspect of enjoying life together, negative emotions will not overpower you, and you will feel the difference in many ways.

4. Self-care

Dealing with emotional cycles begins with taking care of yourself. You have to have a healthy body to feel well each day. It is essential that you take care of your health because we are not guaranteed to have healthy bodies all the time. If you feel tired, or sick, these can negatively impact your emotions.

Emotional intelligence can help in relationships because you begin to take care of your health and overall well-being. As much as possible, you avoid any stresses, anger, or even depression to get in the way.

Having good self-care is going to be an essential part of your routine, and it will impact how you feel in social situations. In the workplace, it will affect how productive you are, because if you feel good about yourself and your appearance, you will exude more confidence and project that assertiveness onto others. Having good hygiene, getting the proper exercise, and eating well will be ways that you can take care of yourself, and you will feel much better when you interact with others at the workplace.

Self-care will be especially important to you as a leader because you will be delegating tasks, holding meetings and conferences, and other jobs that demand a significant amount of your time and energy. Therefore, it is crucial that you find time to take care of yourself, because this will influence your emotions and how you behave and interact with others at the company.

5. *Worry Less*

To avoid being caught in the trap of a negative emotion that can disarm you, you should focus on the positive and practice uplifting self-talk that will enable you to get out of anxious or worrisome thought patterns. Admittedly, we have a lot to worry about in our lives, whether that is in finances, relationships, customers, or a number of other things. When you worry less about stuff, you will have less emotional responses that are negative to the various difficult emotions that we face.

6. Notice When Your Emotions Start to Get Out of Hand

When you start to feel the problematic emotions overflowing, you should respond to the situation. As we have suggested, you should journal about these experiences and write down all that you are feeling at a given time. Remember how you react to different situations and recall how you were able to solve different situations before. Then, you can correct your emotional response to things later on.

7. Let Go

Another benefit of emotional intelligence in relationships is that it teaches you to let go. As humans, we often become entangled in our emotional cycles and can't manage to pull ourselves out of it. Rather than letting go when we hold a grudge against someone, we hold onto it and clutch it like a death-grip on a steering wheel of a car. However, letting go from an adverse emotion is going to enable you to release the stress of a given situation and manage your response to a negative scenario, and then, you won't feel like you need to respond to every little thing. Here are some steps that you can follow with that.

Observe your feelings without judging them. See how the situation comes about. Say to yourself: "I am feeling this emotion. I won't feel the same way tomorrow or the next day."

Embrace your emotions. Instead of fighting off the negative feelings, we should embrace emotions as part of our humanity, because it will help you to have a better time at coping.

8. Hit the "Pause" Button

We all get furious over something that does not go our way. That's normal and part of human nature. That said, one thing that you can do in practicing emotional intelligence and self-control is hitting the "pause" button. Observe what is around you and in your immediate surrounding. Take a deep breath and close your eyes before you respond to a given situation. After said pause, you can return to what you are doing and can effectively manage the situation.

For any management situation, it is vital that you have a "pause" button to help you take a time-out before you get emotionally wrapped up in a situation and react negatively or regretfully. Exercising emotional self-control is an essential step to your developing as a person and manager of a company.

There are many different ways you can develop emotional intelligence to benefit relationships and be in charge of your emotions. Emotional regulation is one of the most important things you can do as a leader and as a person because the way you handle your feelings is going to speak volumes about your character and personality to others.

If you're able to contain yourself and emotions, rather than acting on emotional impulses, you will demonstrate a sense of maturity that will be a model to your employees. No one wants to work for the boss, who is moody and scares his subordinates into doing what they need to do. They want to work for someone approachable, friendly, and sensitive to the emotions. As we have mentioned above, emotional intelligence has a higher value over IQ, because when you connect with people, it has more meaning and significance than if you were to be smart and know all the answers. While having the brainpower makes a difference and is useful, it is more important that the manager have the interpersonal skills to resolve conflict, handle various difficult situations, and manage the emotions of the people around him or her.

How do you use emotional intelligence?

Another important factor to consider in emotional intelligence is the value of being coached. Coaching has a lot to do with EI simply because effective coaches make use of emotional intelligence throughout their work. They display this by showing emotional balance and staying calm despite stressing situations. This is also coaches' way to better understand clients' perspectives.

Not all leaders can be a great coach. There has to be:

1. The coach needs to be emotionally intelligent and skilled. Are all the coaches who work in your organization emotionally intelligent? Do they have highly developed self-regard, or do any of them seem to show an 'I'm ok as long as I help others' attitude, reacting strongly if the coaching does not seem to work? Are the coaches genuinely showing a high regard for others, going into the coaching relationship with the intention of helping the person being coached to in some way benefit from the coaching? Do the coaches your organization uses 'empty themselves' of strong emotions before coaching and show high levels of emotional control during the coaching sessions? Are the coaches you use highly attuned to the people they coach, showing high levels of empathy and paying careful attention to visual cues, voice changes, the type of words people use and emotional responses?

2. The person being coached must want to be coached and be ready to change. Are open discussions used to explain what coaching is and how it can be used, and to determine the attitudes towards coaching of the person being coached? Does the coach listen carefully for words or phrases suggesting reluctance to change and low personal power? Phrases like 'I have to', 'I need to', 'I should', 'I suppose I could', and 'I might' all suggest some reluctance or lack of

motivation to change. Are regular reviews and evaluations of the effectiveness of the coaching used to determine what the person being coached thinks about it?

3. The organization where the coaching takes place needs to have a culture suitable for coaching. What changes have recently taken place in your organization and how have they impacted staff morale? What are the absenteeism and staff turnover rates? How much are staff willing to put in extra time and effort for the benefit of the organization? Are clear boundaries and contracts put in place around coaching, covering things like confidentiality, frequency, purpose of coaching and measurement?

This is why more and more companies are offering coach training opportunities, claiming to teach people the essential coaching skills to be able to go and coach others.

The Emotionally Intelligent Coach

There are six leadership styles, and one of them is coaching. Having managers who can coach is deemed by many companies as a big advantage in order to achieve successful people management.

Many companies assume that managers should also do the coaching since they won't be promoted as managers in the first place if they have no idea of the technicalities of the job. Far more important, in order to become effective at coaching, you should know how to manage yourself and your relationship with others as well.

To become effective in coaching, one requirement is a high level of emotional intelligence apart from skills, experience, and knowledge of dealing with and training others. All these make up for an emotionally intelligent coach who will help their subordinates better enhance performance at work.

So how does emotional intelligence linked to coaching? Having the ability to differentiate who you are and what you do is important. Those who are fond of helping others for a profession may choose to do this because of their desire and willingness to help other people. Oftentimes, this is confused with self-regard.

What this means to say is that there are those who only do it for the sake of work, such is called conditional self-regard: "I am fine as long as I help others", "I am doing better as long as I know that I am in control". Both examples are considered low self-regard, and may most probably lead to poor and ineffective management.

If one's self-regard is not fully developed, you tend to make moral judgements of others. You also tend to utter words that are emotionally unintelligent, such as "You are not good enough", "I don't like you". People who have low self-regard often blame other people, point fingers on others, and critical, and judgmental.

So in order to be an efficient coach and make it a point that you know the difference between who you are and what you do, you need to know that you are coaching or leading specifically for the needs of others rather than for your needs.

Recognizing Emotions on Others

In order to become a genuine leader, you must have a high regard for others. When you do, it is easier to accept them for who they are sans the judgement.

Judgement won't make you an effective leader because it only clouds your understanding and often leads to directive leadership. Take for example, if one of your members tell you about something that is far beyond your morals and values, you don't treat that person badly just because you disagree with him or her. And, you don't equate the person as bad just because you don't agree with what he's saying.

High regard for others is all about accepting that there are those people who do what they do simply because those are their beliefs and they are raised to be like that. This doesn't mean you have to agree with them all the time, but it means that you have to be aware of your own values and beliefs, and keep the personal out of the coaching session.

Take for instance saying something wrong about another person. If the one you're coaching said something about another person, a judgmental coach would further question the person about the other details. But, a coach who has high regard for others would accept the information, but would not treat it as a fact until he sees and experiences it first-hand.

To answer such situations in an emotionally intelligent position, you shouldn't lose your core values and respect other's beliefs even if you disagree with them.

To succeed in coaching, do coaches need to be non-directive all the time? Do they need to know the topics for discussion rather than the people under them?

The foundation of successful coaching uses life positions. The coach's main purpose is to always be of support to the individuals under him. While this said support is under non-directive listening and questioning, it may also include a touch of directive ideas for improving and cultivating of thoughts, attitudes, and behaviors.

The coach's attitudes and intentions are just as important as his coaching skills. An emotionally intelligent coach makes use of a combination of skills such as self and other awareness as well as the right know-how to enable the improvement of those under him.

The main aim here is to focus on the people you coach and at the same time aim for your awareness, attitude, and skills.

An emotionally intelligent coach should be both confident and comfortable with who they are and the way they coach people. They believe in their skills and effectiveness to affect the lives of those they influence.

Awareness of others is an important skill required being a leader. You need to be tuned in to your feelings and be conscious of how things affect them in order to become an effective one in your job.

Open communication, developing relationships, and being able to listen on a perceptive and sensitive level is important. Listen not just with your ears, but with your whole body. The greater part of the communication process is non-verbal that involves facial expression, eye contact, volume, and tone of voice. These are more likely to tell you how a person is feeling rather than just listening to what they say.

The human brain is programmed to pick up these non-verbal cues, feel the emotions, and even reflect the behavior.

Types of Coaching

Developing high levels of self and other awareness will let coaches lessen their being subjective and instead be focused on who they are coaching. EI coaches will be tuned in to their own feelings and intuitions, and take advantage of these to understand better the people they are coaching. At the same time, they are also able to manage their emotions and take note of emotional cues sent their way. This will be better for both the coach and the coaches.

There are 3 types of coaching:

1. The other-focused or low self-awareness and high awareness of others.

If you are this type, it means that you focus more on others' feelings with very little attention to their emotional hijacks and intuition. This is considered unproductive because coaches will most probably let their own emotions and judgement get in the way in their coaching style, stopping them from leading in a directive way.

2. The self-focused coach or high self-awareness, low awareness of others.

Self-focused stick to their own program and plan instead of others. When this type of coaching is used, you as a coach tend to miss important cues such as facial expressions, choice of words, tone variations, and body language.

3. The unaware or the low self-awareness, low awareness of others.

Needless to say, this is the most ineffective of all three for very obvious reasons. This type views coaching as a rational kind of pursuit that only focuses on actions and facts, but totally ignoring emotional cues. Coaching from an emotionally unconscious state is like traveling sans the map. It is just a waste of time, ineffective, and could be very dangerous.

Chapter 6 – All about Empathy

Empathy and Example of Empathy

Empathy allows you to understand others effectively enough to connect and deal with them. This is deemed as a salient factor of compassion for others regardless if you know them or not.

Empathy lets you connect with others and understand their feelings, which makes it a vital part in developing good and healthy relationships, social, and emotional skills.

Empathy is also both social and emotional skills that aid us in understanding further people's intentions, emotions, circumstances, and needs, and be able to offer those help, support, and proper perspective.

Empathy is also considered a skill that is strong in some people. They can easily empathize with others, their circumstances, and needs. They are called empaths.

What is an empath? They said that everyone is an empath, regardless if you are aware of it or not. An empath is someone who is conscious of others' needs, their perceptions, and even others' body language.

We're all empathic by nature. This is important in getting your way through the world. Everyone, at some point in their lives, have read intentions, felt emotions, and seen social interactions and dealt with them. This is because empathy is predominant to human being's capability to interact, understand, and connect with others.

The difference between being empathic and being an empath is one of understanding and intent. Words may have propensity to obscure social interaction and the most honest forms of communication. It is believed that there is more to words and there exists in the space between.

Here is an example:

Jenny always knew what it's like to be a video editor, and that involves sitting in front of the computer and figuring out how to make a video more appealing to its would-be viewers. She is the team leader of all video editors in the office. The company has recently hired interns, and she suddenly remembered what it was like and how it felt being an intern because she has experienced it herself. She had squinted at the screen for long periods and sometimes had eye strain that she had to deal with.

Jenny also remembered the time when a client was disappointed in her work all because she forgot to include an important clip. This happened once when she was just starting out and had zero experience of the job. She was mortified at the time and felt complete shame and remorse as a result of the experience. She feared for her career. She thought she might be fired over it. However, her boss told her that it is just part of the job and she can do better next time.

When Tamara was first hired as a video editor, she also do not have any experience in the field just like Jenny. There was a time when a client complained about her work and this has put her in a bad light. Tamara's supervisor recognized it and played the middle man between the two, but she also came to Tamara and said that she needs to follow-up with her about it.

Tamara went to Jenny and told her what happened. Tamara told Jenny how demotivated she is and is planning to just shift career. But with Jenny's gentleness and understanding, she was able to convince Tamara that it will be alright. Her season will shift and that it's not the end of it all. She made her feel a lot better because she had empathy for her.

After that communication, the client came back with a note of understanding that showed empathy also with Tamara. It was a positive resolution to a difficult situation. This type of scenario is an example of empathy. Jenny showed compassion for Tamara because she knew exactly how she felt because she has been there and have done it before. Tamara felt sorry for what she has done, but was able to get better after that episode. All ended well.

Reading Others' Emotions

Reacting to others' emotions is a vital part of how you can make meaningful relationships. However, it is not always helpful. A lot of times, it is quite harmful. For instance, calling somebody hurtful words just because they intentionally made their way to the front of the line even if you came there first would only result to a commotion. Emotional reactions in their worst form can occur in acts that are shameful and harmful. That was an example of the worst kind of emotional response.

Let's put it in another way. How about reacting to other's jokes? Sometimes, people will make jokes or different offensive remarks that can invoke anger in a person and cause a great deal of disagreement among people. Laughing has a way of bringing people together, but it can also be very offensive to some and cause them to react in anger or frustration at the laughing person. This is where learning others' communication styles is very important. It is crucial that you find ways of relating to other people's emotions and sense of humor because that will be the way that you can make friends with others.

Also, you have to understand whenever others are feeling sad and how you can react to their sadness and provide comfort and support to them. In particular, when someone else is having a tough time and needs someone to comfort them, you can provide the necessary support by just simply being there for them. Being a good friend involves sharing in the joys and the challenges as well. It requires maximum emotional sensitivity.

Types of Empathy

1. Physical Empaths

You are especially attuned to other people's physical symptoms and tend to absorb them into your body. You also can become energized by someone's sense of well-being.

2. Emotional Empaths

You generally take up others' emotions and can become a sponge for their feelings. This can either be a happy or sad emotion.

3. Intuitive Empaths

You experience exceptional views and assessments such as messages in dreams, intensified intuition, animal and plant communication, telepathy, and even communication with the other side of the world.

4. Telepathic Empaths

They obtain perceptive information about others at the present time. Telepathic empaths can instinctively read and study what is happening with others in the present time, even if a person's thoughts and feelings are unexpressed. They receive flashes, images, and impressions about loved ones and even complete strangers.

Here's how telepathic empaths can look like: You're thinking about a close friend, and then suddenly, this close friend gave you a call and informed you that her mother died. At the moment you pick up the phone, you immediately knew that something terrible happened.

How can you tell if an intuition is precise and not just a forecast of your own issues and emotions? Take note if the information that you have received has an unbiased or compassionate tone. To stay clear, you must know yourself well. For instance, if a fear of abandonment is an emotional trigger for you and you keep sensing that your partner is going to leave you, you are probably projecting this said fear onto them. But if you get a matter-of-fact flash with an unbiased tone that your coworker is going to resign from work, that vision is most likely accurate. You may be upset afterward because you don't want to lose this person, but the information didn't initially carry an emotional charge.

Being a telepathic empath can be overwhelming. You may not be tuning in intentionally, yet the intuitions still arise. To avoid intuitive overload, shield yourself and stay grounded.

As a telepathic empath, the information you pick up allows you to develop both more insight and compassion for people. You can also help them if there's an opening to do so. It's a gift to feel this heightened connection to others' thoughts and feelings. Respect this gift at all times.

5. Dream Empaths

They are ardent dreamers and receive intuitive information from their dreams that allows them to help other people and guide them in their path. Dream empaths always have vivid dreams that they remember, an experience that frequently starts in childhood. If you're a dream empath, you look forward to sleeping every night and are enticed to the dream world. Dreams are considered to be a powerful form of intuition because they side step the ego and the mind to propose a vivid insightful information. They bring guidance about spirituality, healing, and conquering difficult emotions.

Dreams can also be precognitive or telepathic where you communicate information about current and future issues. You may even dream about what will happen in the next ten years or even have flashes of someone else's dreams when you're talking to the person. This is because empaths are so accustomed and used to their dreams, they have more access to this realm.

There are also dream empaths who have spirit guides that they encounter and communicate with in their dreams. These guides can be in the form of angels, animals, people, or voices. They can lead you to solve a problem, unearth evidences, or overcome problems. Not everyone has specific spirit guides; if you do, be sure to listen to them because they will help you have compassionate information that will help you and others as well. Apart from this, dream empaths also have the ability to travel to other realms in their dreams.

As a dream empath, your abilities can be developed. All you have to do is write down your dreams and keep a journal. When you wake up, don't get up yet. Spend some quiet moments for just a few minutes and make sure to document whatever snatches of your dreams that you remember.

6. Precognitive Empaths

This type of empath often have premonitions about what will happen in the future while they are either in deep sleep dreaming or awake. They can either have these premonitions unexpectedly or when they are purposely tuned in. You may receive premonitions about relationships, your career or someone else's, health, and other life issues. For example, you might know if a loved one or a close friend will get sick or pass away. Precognitive empaths receive this information from nonlocal realms (a storehouse of collective information, which is said to contain all of human history—past, present, and future), and doesn't come from the linear world.

A reminder though that Precognitive empaths should use their ability with integrity. If you happen to have premonitions, you can warn others such as a dangerous occurrence. However, you must be aware that the information you're receiving are just a probability. Meaning to say, there's always a chance you could be wrong. This is why you should learn to sense if the information or premonition you have is appropriate for sharing to others.

Precognitive empaths have many misconceptions about their gift. You may feel you are causing the events you predict or believe it is your responsibility to prevent them, especially deaths. Neither is true. Highly charged negative events and emotions simply emit louder signals. They are easier to sense than happier circumstances for untrained precognitive empaths. As you hone your intuition, you will be able to attune to a wider range of signals.

7. Mediumship Empaths

These empaths can communicate with people, spirits, and animals on the Other Side. They have the ability to bridge the gap between the living and the other side. They also have the ability to communicate with them.

Mediumship is an echo to what lies beyond this world. This empath is deemed as a channel who is able to release their egos and intellectual minds to allow intuitive information to come through them. Mediumship is a skill you can develop with practice and with proper guidance from an experienced and skilled mentor.

If you are this kind of empath, you can communicate to the Other Side by initially opening your heart in a meditative state. Next, identify the person you want to be in touch with, and deeply ask to contact them. Be open to visual, auditory, or other kinds of messages that you will receive. The process is like communicating with anyone else except that this person is pure energy. But just like any other intuitive experiences, you may be overwhelmed with the experience, so be very careful.

To stay calm and centered, it's important to realize that you have the right to say "no" to any experience you don't want. You may need to set your own boundaries. However, the time you start to see it as just a normal broadening of your empathy, it would be easier for you to the set the limits.

8. Plant Empaths

This kind of empath can feel the needs of plants and connect with their essence. Plant empaths have a natural attraction to plants, trees, and flowers. They naturally have an attachment and communicate with plants' spirits. Plant empaths have the power to determine if a plant is healthy or not.

You can hear plants and talk to them. You are also drawn easily to bodies of water, mountains, and woods. You find yourself very close to nature and you enjoy just being outside. You like to climb them, touch them, and hug them that you sometimes even say "hi" to them when you pass by them.

Plant empaths also have a green thumb. When they plant trees and flowers, they flourish and bloom. This is because these plants are drawn to them as well. This mutual feeling makes these vegetation more responsive to their presence and touch. This is the reason why many plant empaths enjoy gardening the most or they enter a field that is related to it such as garden design, floral arranging, farming, landscape architecture, and botany among others. They just feel happy when they are around the natural world.

Plant empaths also become healers, herbalists, or some kind of medicinal practitioners. They would often offer a service of homeopathy or prescribe plant remedies. There are also flower essences that are kept in a bottle to treat different kinds of diseases. During the early years, most people rely on medicinal plants for healing. They treat plants as emotional, responsive, and intelligent. There are also tribal shamans who exist then and now and act as messengers between the spirit world and these plants. They have the ability to tap into the healing capacities of plants.

If you can identify with this type of empath, you feel their divinity and are able to get guidance from them. There is a technique identified by shamans as gazing. They simply look into plants and flowers and they are able to receive information. You can sit beside a plant and ask it any question, meditate, and receive an answer. If you are a plant empath, it's easier for you to hear their messages from spiritual to personal guidance.

The only challenge is that you tend to feel the pain of these greens. You know if they are dying or hurting. You feel deeply hurt when forestry is being destroyed. A plant empath even feels the pain when these trees are harmed. In order for you to release this pain, you must learn how to accept these physical sensations and emotions. Try breathing the negative emotions out of your system and stay on the positive. Also, be open to accepting and giving love and care for the nature.

9. Earth Empaths

If you are an earth empath, you find yourself in harmony with the earth, weather, and even the solar system. Since you are attuned to the earth, you can easily feel the warmness of the sun, brightness of the stars, attractiveness of the moon, and even the power of the storm.

This kind of empath lets you be one with the earth. So anything that happens to it, you also experience and feel. The beauty of the earth sustains you and the health of the earth nourishes you. You are more sensitive to weather changes and experiences seasonal affective disorder. This is a kind of disorder where you feel down when it's raining or during the winter season.

You treat the earth and everything in it, including the universe, as family. The stars and the moon are your acquaintances. There are also those who prefer to just stay all night gazing at the stars rather than partying all night because it gives them the feeling of both happiness and stillness all at the same time. There are those who treat the heavens as their true home. These empaths just knew.

According to earth empaths themselves, there is a need for them to connect to the earth's energy as their form of healing and adjusting to fully dwell in their bodies.

If you're an earth empath, you're happy when the planet earth is protected and you feel bad and hurt when the earth is harmed. You can sense every feeling and emotion felt by the Earth. That's how you are so connected to it.

You often experience premonitions that concern natural calamities and feel it as these natural disasters are happening. There are reported earth empaths who have premonitions just seconds before a natural disaster occurs. Some feel body sensations before an earthquake, while there are those who repeatedly wakes up during sleep before a volcanic eruption. These kinds of premonitions put a great change in your body depending on the kind of natural disaster is occurring. Therefore, it is important that you be aware of this and practice self-care especially when this natural disaster happens.

Earth empaths are also sensitive to sun flares. Magnetic storms have an influence on the earth's magnetic fields and even an earth empath's body. Hurricanes, earthquakes, tornados, and volcanic eruptions occur after a powerful astrophysical activity. During these periods, expect to have heart palpitations, headaches, anxiety, or mood swings. There are also studies connecting solar flares to depression, bipolar episodes, anxiety, and even suicide. It is also believed that uprising, revolutions, and turmoil across the earth are connected to solar flares. For earth empaths, the happenings and the feelings that come with it are amplified in them.

In order to make the most of this ability, it is important that you try to connect to the earth. Make time going outdoors. Spend your time in the woods, mountains, and oceans where you can easily feel the earth elements fill your soul.

It is also important that you maintain a healthy and clean lifestyle to deepen your relationship with the earth. You can effectively ingest the earth's energy by eating the right kind of food sans the junk. Practice Earthling by simply gazing at the stars, walking barefoot, or swimming in the sea or rivers. Just feel the earth's presence so you can let yourself be absorbed in her natural energy.

You can also ask for guidance to the earth. She will give your answers through your intuition. You will know it when she answers. You'll just feel it. Practice earth medicines so you will feel happier, whole, and healthier.

10. Animal Empaths

Animal empaths have the capacity to communicate with animals and feel their feelings. Are you aware of dog whisperers? They are examples of animal empaths. If you're one, it means that you can easily identify with animals' feelings, health, and emotions. You know when they are happy and healthy, and when they're sad and sick. It is by being fully aware of their feelings that you can be able to help them in their healing.

Also, an animal empath easily attracts animals. You will immediately know it because when they are near, animals are drawn to their presence. It's like these animals just know that they are safe in your presence.

Animal empaths are usually found in animal shelters, entering veterinary school, and are also animal advocates. It is like their main goal in life is to be of support and rescue animals.

There are a lot of animal empaths in the olden days. One perfect example is Saint Francis of Assisi. He talks to animals and even tamed a wolf. When he is around, animals flock to him. No wonder he is the patron of all animals. He loved being surrounded by animals and even went for periods of isolation with only animals to accompany him.

When you are an animal empath, you have this unexplainable love for them. It is a different kind of love that these animals also begin to pick up the emotions. These animals in return are highly empathic and could also sense if you are sad or happy. Take for instance, dogs. They know when their owner is happy or not. They know when their human is not around the house. They simply sense it. How much more if you're an animal empath.

You can also get intuitive assistance from animals. They can give you warnings, premonitions, and even good luck. Native people believed that animals could hear a person's thoughts and if you are an animal empath, you sure will hear theirs, too.

In summary, there are many kinds of empaths; all have wonderfully and diverse nuanced level of compassions. You may be one or more of these types of empaths. As you discover what empath you are and identify your gifts, you will realize that this ability does not only help in enriching one's life, but can also be used to help other people.

Why Become More Empathic – Importance of Empathy

The empath's journey is considered an exciting adventure. In short, there are a lot of things to be grateful for. There is an unexplainable sense of joy and compassion within you. You are able to comprehend things at a much deeper level. Your level of understanding is simply tremendous.

When you're an empath, you are attuned to the energy and beauty of life. Your level of compassion is so great that you long to help others and make them feel better all the time. You are not cold-hearted. Your sensitivities and kindliness let you be more vulnerable, caring, and being.

If you are an empath, you have this very special connection with nature. You feel an affinity with trees, plants, animals, mountains, stars, and clouds. You are drawn to the vastness yet quietness of the desert, the depths of the sea, the majestic canyons and mountains, and the peace of the forests. You know how to be one with nature. You enjoy what nature gives you. You can dance under the moonlight and feel her presence. You simply have this goal in life – to protect nature, the earth, and preserve precious resources.

As empaths, you have the ability to positively influence your family and friends. You are the breaker of chains of negativity whether in the workplace or inside the home. Although you don't voluntarily ask to be the one to do this, but instead, it is said to be your purpose to fulfill this. The moment empaths honor their sensitivities, they are refusing patterns of addiction, abuse, and neglect. Through the acceptance of this gift, you have become a channel to strengthen family ties and repair what's damaged in the familial whole. Mindful, emotionally intelligent, and empathic people are more often than not the best agents of this change.

Moving toward the Light

The earth is filled with both suffering and joy. An empath's role and importance is to use sensitivity to somehow tip the balance and help for a greater good. Empaths are considered to be soldiers of the light. They're not afraid of darkness and they have so much belief in their compassion.

Empaths are expected to nurture the world's vibration. People are better off and become good ones when they are surrounded with empaths who have a positive yet sensitive energy, loving, and string. Even children can pick these kinds of traits.

The only challenge for an empath is fear. Afterall, you are still human and it is but normal to feel fear. But, it is your goal to get over this fear and eventually heal it. You have to overcome your fear or else, you will block your way toward the light.

When you are able to conquer your fear, you become stronger, and this represents a new example of leadership. You are able to advocate mutual understanding and lead others to the path of peace. And, this can only be done when you lead through emotional and spiritual work. Through an empath's sensitivity, one is able to produce a compassion revolution and change the world for the better.

As one of the environmentalists said, the planet earth no longer needs successful people residing in it. While their contributions are helpful, what this planet needs are restorers, lovers, healers, peacemakers, and storytellers. It needs people to actually live their lives and fulfill their purpose here on earth. They need people who upholds moral values. They need people who are courageous. They need people who have compassion with others and to the Earth. All these qualities do not speak of success as what the society defines.

Empaths are key to displaying this big shift. It is with their sensitivities where there is nonviolence. If you keep your sensitivities open, empaths can become restorers and healers, and lovers and seers. Therefore, it is a must that you always be centered in your power. Don't be fearful of who you really are. Do what you need to do, and do it well. Do it for the greater good without walking on other people, and the rest will follow.

Commit to this goal and don't be too affected by this fast-paced world. The speeding of time will only rush you. The busyness of life will only stress you. What you need is to take on a compassionate stand. The more empowered and inspired you are, the more you can express the change needed by this world.

Learn to Celebrate Your Gifts

This is one of the importance of empathy. You should be always grateful for what you have. As you go through life, just continue on clarifying the ways that your being an empath helps you, other people, and the whole of it.

Here are some exercises to help you with just that:

Embrace Your Empathy

It is beneficial to be empathic. This could help you in more ways than one. This is why it would be best to take a moment to ponder on the goodness and the many benefits being one could bring your life:

- Remember the moment when you chose to listen to your intuition and immediately know what to do? It is by listening to that little voice that you are able to make sound decisions, pick the right job, get into the right relationship, and live the best life possible.

- Remember the moment when you were able to show empathy to your spouse? It helped greatly in deepening your relationship with each other and you learned a lot of good things about one another.
- Remember the moment when you were so worried about something and you just don't know what to do next? Instead of wallowing in your fears and thinking of the worse that might happen, you show compassion to yourself. You didn't obsess with the fear. Rather, you found a way to resolve it. This showing of self-love is a vital attitude to display especially when faced with challenges.
- Remember the moment when a friend experienced an awful heartbreak? You were there to give your helping hand and stayed with her no matter what.
- Remember how as an educator, a boss, a leader, or a parent, you were able to inspire a child to be more aware of his sensitivities? Inspiring a child to enhance this skill is something life-changing. Be proud of yourself.

The Path to Inner Peace

In the process of knowing yourself and embracing your sensitivities, know that the road to inner peace, self-acceptance, and overall growth is not that easy. The road will be bumpy most of the time. You will find yourself going back to same old issues, only that this time, the truths are revealed thereby developing your self-knowledge.

But this makes the journey more exciting. You yearn to find your inner peace, so you move closer to the light. You delve deeply into the bumpy road of life, and self-love and high regard to oneself help you triumph over these trials. You'll be put in a situation where you will feel stretched, but the outcome will be more radiant and more connection to your inner peace and spirit. Now, there is none more precious than achieving just that.

With this kind of mindset, it is easier to conquer your fears and enjoy your life journey. As you go along with life, each day, reflect on the changes that have occurred to you. See how your life has changed so far and how your relationships have improved from the time you have embraced fully your being an empath.

Given this, you need to make sure that every victory, big or small, is celebrated. Assert you needs, listen to your intuition, and center yourself even in the middle of disorder.

Be comfortable in the thought that you are no longer chained to what others think about you. You say yes to yourself not because you think others would be comfortable about it. Celebrate your capacity to finally love and accept yourself without second-guessing. Be grateful for every baby step you've made. Celebrate your progress. Don't be afraid when you backslide. We are all inclined to experience that. But you should remember that in every situation, no matter how challenging, always treat yourself with kindness and compassion.

As an empath, it is part of your purpose in this world to return to humanity what is humane and just. This is your share in the countercultural revolution. The world is already full of cruel people, I applaud you for being brave and courageous and standing for what is right. I applaud you for being authentic in a world full of fakes. And I applaud you for not giving up on the world, believing that it has so much to offer.

Take note of this: everybody is part of a big empath family in this universe. This means that everyone is interconnected with each other and shares a common goal even if we have our own differences and purposes in life. So allow kindness to draw in you and be able to share it with others. Take comfort knowing that our hearts are connected to each other no matter the distance. We may not have met yet, but as an empath, there is this part in our being that says we are one.

How to Leverage Positive Emotions in People

As an empath, you should be comfortable enough in your working environment to make you feel happy and fulfilled. However, since most empaths may find it hard to manage stress effectively given their skills, it is a bit challenging for them to recover without being exhausted from their work.

Empaths are artists, inventors, creators, visionaries, and the kind of individuals who feel first. They are able to see the bigger picture of things as they go their way through their workday, every day. They are outside the box thinkers and often find company and organizational office setup more restrictive for their talents and skills. This is the reason why you will notice that when you step into an artist's office or creators' workplace, the setting is not typical like that of an office environment. The difference in interior design and setup likewise help fuel their creativity. And once their talents are tapped, their jobs can be really energizing, fulfilling, and definitely worth it.

Empaths often succeed in their jobs. They also become leaders and thrive given the right work environment. A kind of job that matches an empath's temperament motivates them, places them in a creative zone, and fires their passion. A simple act of kindness gives an empath a fulfilling feeling knowing that they have somehow created a difference and contributed something good to others. That's what an empath heart is. Always giving, always feeling, and always willing to share more.

The wrong work, however, can pull the life right out of these empaths and could set off a pouring of physical and emotional symptoms as a reaction to emotional overload and stress.

How does an empath thrive in a work environment? There are actually three major factors that contribute to this. The sense one gets from working, the energy of the people around them, and the energy of their own space. Know where you stand here and start visualizing how you want your situation to change and improve.

1. The Sense One Get at Work

Empaths are concerned about what they can get from working. They are looking for a deeper sense of meaning in what they do that would actually sync with their sensitivities. They always like to feel that they have somehow made a difference, big or small, to someone else's life. This work does not need to be grand. You can be anything like running a business, gardening, farming, healthcare professions, and the like. What's important is that the job feels right in your body and won't easily sap your energy or drain you.

Many are blessed to have found the kind of job they love. So if you're still stuck at something you think always drains your energy, go find something that will bring you to life once more and will make you want to do it over and over again.

And because empaths are mostly leaders, you have the power to influence your subordinates not to be stuck in the rut. Do what you love best and you'll surely find meaning in what you do. Take the courage to follow your intuition and what your heart dictates.

As an empath, you surely know what you really want in life, all you have to do is be brave in pursuing the right career for you.

For those who seek meaning in their work, it pays to know the values of good service and love for what you do. This can help clarify meanings. Also, it pays to always be grateful in whatever your job can offer you instead of constantly complaining about something that you disapprove of. This will help you set a constructive and positive environment, whether or not you choose to stay in the job or not. Doing this will allow you to make sound decisions for your life and career.

2. The energy of the people around

The people around you can make or break the level of comfort you have at work. Sensitive people are said to have lower tolerance for conflict, chaos, and even office politics. The constant office drama disturbs an empath and make them more anxious and drained.

Sensitive people do better in a friendly environment that has strong support system, collaboration, and goodwill. This is why competitive and high-adrenaline kind of job is not an ideal job for an empath.

Ideally, empaths want to feel that they really fit in the job especially when dealing with their bosses and coworkers. They would often look for empaths like themselves in the workplace for them not better relate. Although not all people are empaths and display a positive attitude and outlook in life, it's still a good start that one gravitates to other empaths.

In the workplace, there will always be energy zappers or what they call energy vampires. These are often passive-aggressive, narcissists, chronic talkers, victims, drama kings and queens, and rageaholics. Just about any kind of workplace has these people lurking around. They are toxic to be with, they often complain, they always want to be involved in office dramas, and always have a negative thing to say about everything. They can be so destructive that empaths can develop health issues such as irritability, stress, fatigue, pain, and aggravation.

In order to prepare yourself for this kind of situation, here are those who just shrug off whatever is being told to them by an energy vampire or just do their own thing. Empaths who encounter this kind of people just fully devote their time and effort by either shifting their schedules or just focusing more on their tasks.

It is highly advised that you apply some protection techniques such as learning to say "no", meditating, and setting boundaries in order for you to take good care of yourself in the workplace. This will help you lessen energy depletion or if not completely avoid it. Empaths often better off spend most of their time mingling with positive people at work, because believe me, there are still a lot of them out there. People who uplift, encourage, and motivate you, they are your people.

3. The energy of their own space

Every nook and cranny of an office building has its own energy. There are spaces that are enriching and light, while there are those that drain the energy and are depressing. Empaths have the ability to intuit and perceive the energy of these spaces given their developed sensitivities.

It is advised that you be familiar with the energy of your workplace and know if it feels light or not. There are also times when there is what you call a leftover energy from previous residents of a workplace, building, or even residential homes. If you feel that something is off in a particular area, you can help cleanse the area by spraying rose water.

Also, you can try meditation in the area where you feel something is off. This will help infuse it with positive energy and eliminate any form of negativity. You can do this alone or with people whom you can trust in the workplace who understand you.

Empaths are also sensitive to things that add to the feeling of a particular space. This consists of activity levels, the noise in the place, privacy, smell, the lighting, air flow, and even proximity.

Empaths are very sensitive to light and don't do well with little spaces. They prefer large perimeters to keep stresses and negativities away from them. They also do not want cluttered rooms because these deplete the energy. They like spacious, clean, and serene rooms where they can meditate and just enjoy the stillness and calmness of the space.

Electronic devices that are very close could also drain the energy of empaths. This is often called "electro-sensitives". The radiation that comes from computers and cellphones affect the electromagnetic fields around the heart and brain.

Finally, the energy coming from the people around you also have an immediate effect to how the workplace feels. A workplace filled with negative people are heavy to the feeling, is usually dark, and has this limiting effect. Whereas, a work setting filled with positive people are colorful, light to the feeling, and creates a happy and serene environment.

Emotional Contagion at Work

The problem with empaths is that they can easily absorb negative energy and stress in their working environment. When emotional contagion happens to them, it spreads like a virus, lowers employees' morale, and ultimately affect everybody's productivity.

The good news is, happiness is also contagious and can easily spread in the workplace provided that there are more positive and happy people around. This affirmative emotional contagion yields happy employees, increased productivity, and improved cooperation at work. Although this feeling can be felt by everyone, this feeling is amplified in empaths. Yes, they can either easily pick up negative vibes, but at the same time, the happy ones.

Remember, you become what you surround yourself with. This is why most empaths are very careful when it comes to choosing whom to be with people. But since they have this innate feeling of being drawn to anyone, regardless if they are good or bad, they easily become connected to them.

To somehow find the balance, empaths need to know some self-care tips to prevent you from energy zappers, emotionally demanding, and negative kind of work setting:

1. Always take a break – when everything seems to becoming more overwhelming for you, it will help to give yourself a break of at least 5-10 minutes. This will help clear the mind, stretch your body, and remove you from the stress even for just a while. Not taking a break will often lead to burnout and also contributes to not being productive at all.

2. Create a comfortable and clutter-free workspace. A tidy desk helps you think clearly and make sound decisions. You can place a small plant on your desk and some

inspirational sayings. A clutter-free desk reduces stress and facilitates creativity.

3. Don't overstretch yourself. Limit the number of tasks and clients you have in a day. You can't do it all no matter how hard you try. Do not squeeze in one task after the other because chances are, you'll be overwhelmed for the rest of the day. Reschedule if you can other appointments on days when you don't have too many work to do.

4. Practice deep breathing. Mindful deep breathing increases energy level, clears out negativity, detoxifies the body, and improves blood flow.

5. Don't skip meals. Try to eat as much healthy food as possible. Avoid too much carbs or those that are considered quick fix meals. Try to bring your own healthy snacks wherever you go so you won't be tempted to drive thru fast food chains.

6. Set boundaries at work. One way of protecting yourself from energy zappers is to learn the art of saying "no". If you think you can't do it and can't help them, say no. Do not force yourself to do something just so you can please them. Also, if you're a leader, do not always say "yes" to your members. Stand your ground and apply the rules of the company at all times so you will be taken seriously.

7. Fill your workspace with heart energy. Every day is an opportunity to fill your heart chakra. It is found in the

center of your chest. Feel the heart energy flow through your body for balance. In so doing, the loving energy will flood and fill the room. It infuses a workplace with positivity. This technique is generally used to design a loving environment even in the workplace.

8. Detoxify with water. In order to wash away stress, take a shower or Epsom baths to wash away all the negativities and stresses brought by the day. Also, make sure to hydrate yourself at all times.

9. Shield yourself. When faced with a difficult situation or you're picking up the negative energy of another person, imagine having a white shield of light protecting you. This strategy will help especially if your profession requires constant mingling with different kinds of people with heavy emotions. Shielding doesn't moderate your sensitivities. Instead, it prevents you from picking up anxiety and stress of other people around you.

10. Have fun with nature. Nature has its special healing power that removes all worries, stress, and anxieties. Rather than thinking of your work, be fully occupied with nature during your off time.

The more you use these strategies, the more strengthened and empowered you will become.

The Difference between Empathy and Sympathy

Empathy is feeling different sentiments and emotions of others. It is a means in which a person can fully understand, accept, and identify with the person who is experiencing an emotion.

Take for instance the feeling of losing a loved one. Since you've been in that situation before, it puts you in that opposition where you can relate and be able to offer your counsel and support to the person.

Empathy includes shared experiences where a person feels the pain of another in order to absolutely identify with the situation and the emotions of another. When somebody tells you, "I feel you." Or "I know the feeling", it simply means that they have identified themselves in your situation. That is a sign of empathy.

Another example is a friend in deep debt and has no means to pay for them. You, as an empath, have already experienced the same situation before. So you immediately identified with the situation and offer your help.

You feel empathy for your friend because you have been through the same situation. Consequently, you can identify with the feelings and emotional responses of your friend. This puts you in the best position to comfort and restore your friend. Thus, you help him out by lending him some money.

On the other hand, sympathy is when a person identifies a person's feelings of distress or suffering but is unable to know what a person is going through. It is somewhat like compassionate pity for someone wherein a person may feel sorry for another but also comforts them. At the same time, they don't have the actual life experience that enables them to understand fully what that person is going through emotionally.

An example is a doctor who is giving care to a patient who is suffering from cancer. Doctors have to be emotionally sensitive and aware to be competent and supportive caregivers.

Conclusion

I would like to thank you and congratulate you for reading this book from start to finish.

I hope this book has helped you know more about the different aspects that must be considered in becoming an effective and emotionally intelligent leader.

Leadership may not be for all, but it can also be learned as long as you have the desire in your heart to lead people and be a good influence to them.

The next step is to try to implement the concepts and ideas you have learned from this book especially if you are looking into becoming a leader someday. All it takes really is self-discovery. Once you have discovered that you can lead and the kind of leadership you wish to implement, it is going to be easier as you go along the way.

I wish you the best of luck!

DR. Felicity Gray